The Little Book of Emotional Intelligence

The Little Book of Emotional Intelligence:

How to Flourish in a Crazy World

Andy Cope AND Amy Bradley

First published in Great Britain in 2016 by John Murray Learning.
An Hachette UK company.

This edition published 2018

British Library Cataloguing in Publication Data: a catalogue record for this title is available from the British Library.

2

Hardback ISBN: 9781473636347
Paperback ISBN: 9781473636354
eISBN: 9781473636361

Designed and set by Amy Bradley

Printed and bound in Great Britain by CPI Group (UK) Ltd, Croydon, CR0 4YY

John Murray Learning policy is to use papers that are natural, renewable and recyclable products and made from wood grown in sustainable forests. The logging and manufacturing processes are expected to conform to the environmental regulations of the country of origin.

Carmelite House
50 Victoria Embankment
London EC4Y 0DZ

www.hodder.co.ukk

CONTENTS

Chapter 1

Real-world intelligence

Ahoy!

In which we start with a spine-tingler before visiting hell via a 1970s TV quiz show. We study pirates and various breakfast cereals before looking at the modern nuclear family. We get to grips with the oddity that your host has a mental age of eight as well as a Ph.D. in happiness, before turning to Barbie, magic tricks and dog poo.

I ask you, dear reader, what more could you want from an opening chapter? But, before we kick off, I know what you're thinking – 'Andy, could we have a short introduction about the meaning of life...?'

A meaningful thought

'Sir, I was assisting my 16-year-old daughter with her homework when she received a text from her mum that read, "What do you want from life?"'

'We pondered this profound and somewhat unexpected question. And we debated furiously. Wealth, happiness, health? Or love perhaps?'

'Five minutes later she received another text. "Sorry, predictive text got in the way. I meant 'Lidl'."'

Letter in the *Daily Telegraph*

Begin with the end in mind

DEAD people

...they're everywhere!

There's a creepy line of dialogue in the movie *The Sixth Sense* where the haunted young boy tells Bruce Willis: 'I see dead people.' I think it's the matter-of-factness that makes it so chilling. The poor lad has an unfortunate gift for seeing ghosts.

I think I have a similar 'gift', except that the people aren't physically dead. But there are thousands of them and I see them every day. People going about their lives in a zombie-like trance of mediocrity. Technically, they are alive. There's a pulse. But they're not really living. They're crammed onto the London Underground system, cheek to armpit, earphones and books blocking out reality. Or, outside on the streets, they're jammed into the oxymoronic 'rush hour', grumbling about the traffic without realizing that they *are* the traffic. The living dead are sleepwalking through life, counting down the days until the weekend or their next holiday. Too many people are having a near-life experience.

So, before I begin in earnest, let me give you a statistic. The average lifespan is 4,000 weeks. It's interesting that if you announce that to a crowd of schoolchildren there's a lot of jumping and cheering – 'Woo-hoo, thanks for telling us, Andy. That's like ... for ever!'

But if I announce it to an adult audience there is less punching of the air and more of a collective gulp. Some people reach for their phones, tapping at the calculator to assess how many they have left. Of course, 4,000 weeks is an approximation. It equates to 28,000 days, give or take. A further problem is that, chances are, your weeks are zipping by in a blur.

I've been having a recurring nightmare about Jim Bowen. For the younger generation, Jim was the best game-show host ever. He fronted *Bullseye*, a Sunday-teatime darts-based extravaganza, in which working-class folk from Wolverhampton, say, could win a car, a caravan or, on a good day, a speedboat. It was one of those shows that was so bad it was good because, invariably, the show ended on a downer. The plucky contestants failed to win the top prize and Jim would sidle centre stage and hand over a few quid and a cuddly toy. Jim had one of those well-worn faces that did deadpan sincerity better than any other game-show host. As he consoled the crestfallen contestants he'd stick the boot in. Kick 'em while they're down, Jim, why don't you? The stage would rotate to reveal this week's top prize – the exact thing that they *weren't* going home with – and Jim would utter the best catchphrase in the history of British TV: 'Never mind, folks, let's take a look at what you could have won.'

My recurring nightmare isn't about the speedboat; it's about a much bigger prize than that. It's me in a hospital bed, old and knackered, in standard-issue blue-and-white striped pyjamas, wrinkles etched on my face. I have a tube up my nose and a bag of bright-orange wee hanging from my bedside. It's by no means a pretty dream. I suspect that the end is near. Worse still, in my dream there's a sadness about me. The wrinkles aren't etched from laughter. I've led a mediocre life of working too hard, saving my happiness for weekends and holidays. I've missed too many school plays and bedtime stories. I've been impatient when my grandkids visited and messed up my house. I've moped on rainy days. I've spent too much time with my Facebook friends and not enough time with my flesh-and-blood ones. I've not jumped in enough puddles or made nearly enough sandcastles. I've never been to Sri Lanka or managed to get a ticket for Wales v England at the Millennium Stadium. Life's been long stretches of nothingness interspersed with some cracking holidays. As I lie in my hospital bed, I have an overwhelming sense that life has been distinctly 'OK'. And Jim Bowen's face looms into my nightmare, large and sincere. And he utters his immortal catchphrase, 'Never mind, Andy,' he consoles. 'Shall we look at what you could have won?'

I suspect that death itself isn't the problem. It might be a bit scary, all that 'not breathing', but it's not death that's the source of our mortal anguish, rather the fear that we might not have lived quite the joyous and ebullient go-getting life that we might have. For the truly righteous folks, the reward for a good life seems fairly dull – all that eternal sitting around on clouds listening to harp recitals. If you've led a bad life, you're probably not actually that afraid of the burning for all eternity. The chances are that you've lived a bit and all your mates will be down there with you.

So the 'very good' and 'very bad' are sorted. It's the rest of us who are petrified! Four thousand earthly weeks of mediocrity is such a terrible waste of time!

The aim is to make this an uplifting read. I want to give you some content that inspires and rejuvenates your thinking and your life. So why start with such a sobering thought? Depressing even? Because there's a massive difference between 'being alive' and 'living'. One is rather black and white, requiring nothing more than a pulse. This second one requires what I call 'intelligent living' and it requires a heart and brain.

If you apply the intelligence, it leads to a full-colour high-definition surround-sound life.

$$\heartsuit + \text{Brain} = \text{Intelligent living}$$

Heart   Brain

The pirate within

Your brain loves certainty, which is why you develop habits. Your mind craves consistent patterns, and when life falls outside our normal routine we get scared. So we play safe by making sure that we never have to step outside our routine. We think the same thoughts and live the same days. Those days become weeks and the sameness stretches into months and, hence, life becomes very safe and rather dull.

...Thinking inside the box:

'How we spend our days is how we spend our lives.'

Annie Dillard

But if we open up our minds to change, that means we have to move position. Change means walking away from standing in the middle of 'what you already know' and following the path towards the edge of 'what's possible'. That requires you to be curious enough to stand on the edge of knowledge and, yes, it can be a little scary, but it's also where you learn and grow.

Part of the fear comes from daring to be a little bit different, and by 'different' I mean standing out for the right reasons – a bit more positive, confident, optimistic, happy, vivacious and energetic than the norm. Yes, you've got to be brave enough to stand out, but can you think of anyone who has changed the world by fitting in?

Without wanting to sound too 'up myself', the knowledge in this book has challenged me up to and well beyond my preconceived view of 'what's possible'. That is to say that the old version of me would have poo-pooed some of the ideas in this book, particularly Chapters 7 and 8, which represent a 'Big Bang' of academia, philosophy and common sense that had, until recently, eluded me. I was happy with what I knew and my life was absolutely, steadfastly, resolutely 100 per cent fine. And yours might be too. But if you want to leave the scrubland of 'fine' and upgrade to the mountain pastures of 'awesome', 'brilliant' or 'world class', then I would be delighted to be your tour guide.

But before I grab my umbrella and call for your attention, let me ask a question: 'What is your default setting – Setting 1, "passive bystander" or Setting 2, "active and engaged"?'

your tour guide (aka Andy!)

Personally, I think we're born with the factory default of Setting 2. I don't know any child who sits passively on their first birthday, surrounded by crinkly wrapping paper, looking bored. They toss the toys aside and get stuck into crinkling, tearing and eating the stuff. And what about the boxes the toys came in? Well, they're now a rocket or pirate ship – 'Hoist the mainsail, Jim lad.'

I'm sure there's not a single child who, aged 11 months, attempted to walk, fell on to their backside and thought, 'I give up. Walking's just not my thing.' When I go to the park with my four-year-old niece it's a massive adventure and she insists on jumping in every puddle and chasing every duck. She has rosy cheeks, sparkly eyes, infinite curiosity and oodles of glee. Sure, it might be partly fuelled by her chocolatey breakfast cereal, but what if it runs a bit deeper than that? What if we all have access to that inner source of inspiration and energy? To mix my breakfast cereal metaphors, your internal snap, crackle and pop shows on the outside in the fabled Ready Brek glow.

And then, somewhere along the line, we become inert and uninterested. We feel flat, maybe even a little lost. We end up feeling like cereal that's been swimming in milk for too long and our snap, crackle and pop has been silenced. Life isn't awful – it's just not quite as thrilling as it used to be. Scientists call it 'habituation' and the erosion of passion is so gradual that you often don't notice. Your work isn't quite as exciting; your partner isn't quite as attractive; everything on TV is rubbish. And because we think the world happens from the outside in, we set about renewing things 'out there' – new job, new partner and ... Netflix – that should do it.

David Hare describes it as 'painting over the rust'.[1] We're brightening things up on the outside to cover up the decay on the inside. The solution is temporary.

But hang on. If we are born 'active and engaged', surely that's our default position? So, I ask you: when did jumping in a cardboard box with a West Country cry of 'Hoist the mainsail!' become inappropriate? Can you remember the exact time when jumping in puddles became a bad idea? When did you last use the cushions to build a den in the lounge? When did you last go to the park and chase the ducks, squealing with glee?

factory default

I appreciate that human beings are incredibly

complex animals but have you noticed how when a complicated piece of technology goes wrong it always has a button that sets it back to its factory default? What if we could do the same? Perhaps fun, giggly and playful, and 'Walk the plank, yer rotten scoundrel' is our factory setting, but somehow we forgot along the way. Surely, that would mean that personal development is dead in the water and all you'd need is a huge spoonful of 'personal remembering'.

I spend a lot of time in organizations trying to fix people and teams who have had some vastly overcomplicated restructure or culture change initiative that hasn't worked. At worst, there has been no behaviour change and, at best, the temporary uplift has soon migrated backwards, towards the 'norm'. It's the same with self-help books. If they worked, we'd all be suntanned, super-slim billionaires, running our business empires from a yacht moored in a Monaco marina. The trouble – ALWAYS – is that we gravitate to whatever it is that represents our norm.

personal remembering?

So the only real way to create *sustainable* change is to reset the norm.

Let me pose some mightily big questions for the pirate within. If you had a 'reset' button, would you want to press it and, more to the point, would you be brave enough to press it?

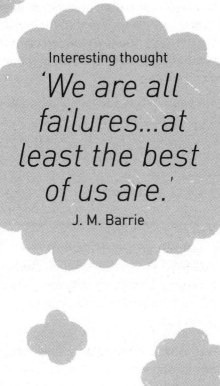

Interesting thought

'We are all failures...at least the best of us are.'

J. M. Barrie

The nuclear option

Let me introduce myself: my name is Andy and I'm from a city in 'Middle England' called Derby. I have a bizarre triple life as a children's author, trainer and researcher. First up, kids' stuff. I'm very proud of my Spy Dog series for Puffin. There are 20 books in the series, which is aimed at seven to ten-year-olds. So, good news – I'm a big kid.

In a jarring juxtaposition of literary styles, I have also spent the past ten years studying the science of happiness, culminating in a Ph.D. from one of England's finest universities (at least, that's what it says on the brochure). Take it from me, that is a very odd combo that places me in a very small part of a Venn diagram. There are an awful lot of 'serious academics' and not very many 'not-so-serious' ones. This book gives me a chance to cross over and to mix the clever stuff with a bit of childlike energy. Or, at least, that's the intention. After ten years of research and 100,000 words, I guess I can best be described as a 'recovering academic'?

I adore the kids' stuff because the writing has to be simple, adventurous, energetic and downright fun. Kids won't tolerate any slackening of the pace so there really is no messing – it's full-on action, adventure and belly laughs from page 1. And then there's the Ph.D., the polar opposite. It feels as though I'm writing in some sort of encrypted code that mere mortals will never be able to decipher. If children's books are so exciting you can't sleep, my thesis is the antidote – a soporific giggle-free tome of academic turgidity. Gags, fluidity and energy are heinous crimes, punished by my supervisor giving me one of her withering looks.

While scrabbling through the academic undergrowth I've spotted some very well camouflaged gems of learning and this book gives me an opportunity to point them out to you. This book is less about telling you what to do. If you're reading a book that has 'Emotional Intelligence' in the title, then I'm guessing that you might already be at the brighter end of the scale (although, to be fair, it's got pictures, so you might have been attracted by them).

The only 'problem' I have in writing a book about emotional intelligence is that I don't see it as a discrete subject; it has octopus-like tentacles that reach into and borrow from positive psychology, neuro-linguistic programming (NLP), appreciative inquiry, 'flourishing' and transformational leadership (to name a few).

My aim is to draw from them all and reveal, as simply as possible, how your mind/body/emotion connection works. I'll aim to throw in a few things that make me chuckle but, more than that, the aim is to challenge your thinking. In particular, to challenge you to *think* about your thinking, with a view to generating some new understanding and to apply yourself differently.

So what is emotional intelligence? That depends on who you ask! There are hundreds of books, all of which are variations on a theme. If you asked me, I'd say it's this:

'Emotional intelligence is the ability to make healthy choices based on accurately identifying, understanding and managing your own feelings and those of others.'

Andy would say...

I'll cover this in more detail later on but for now, simplifying it to the bare bones, emotional intelligence is about tuning in to people, starting with the most important person of all – you.

One of my mates makes me chuckle by suggesting he has a nuclear family.

'Ah, that's nice,' I reply, thinking 'close-knit' as in *The Waltons*. I'm picturing hearty meals of pumpkin pie before a cheery 'Night, Jim Bob' at lights out.

'No!' he says. 'By "nuclear" family I mean we explode a lot and there's a massive amount of fallout. And that fallout can linger for ages.'

In terms of content, I want the material to apply across all domains of your life. I am guessing work is important to you and I'm confident that you will learn things that you can apply in your career. But the biggest results for me have been at home, trying to be a better dad and a half-decent husband.

- Andy found the BIGGEST
- results at
- home!

I myself am made entirely of flaws, stitched together with good intentions

Augusten Burroughs

Scoop your poop

I love the fact that among the original Barbie's phrases was the sentence: 'Math class is tough.' Sadly, in later models, this was deleted, but if you have any sense of political incorrectness left intact, that's very funny. I bet Ken had the equivalent:'I'm home, honey. Where's my dinner?'

This delicious naughtiness was unquestioned until about the mid-1980s. Recently, in the big theatrical production called 'life', the actors have been encouraged to venture from their traditional scripts. What I'm struggling to say is that I'm a white hetero Derby County–supporting male, dragged up in the 1970s playing British Bulldog and riding my bike with no helmet. I have all the baggage associated with that. That's who I am. I can't help being me. I think the Barbie thing is funny.

You are you, with your own baggage. I won't judge if you don't.

REMINDER

Imagine your future self, just a week or so away. The one who has *You're already this!* read this book and made some changes – a glowing, effervescent, bubbling cauldron of glee who has discovered the source of emotional enlightenment. Because, although that previous sentence is kind of cool, and has never been written in the English language before, it sums you up. On a good day, that is. So, this book, in line with all my other books, is not about reinventing yourself. It's not about personal transformation or morphing into a superhero. It's not really about new stuff at all; it's about reminding you of some very simple old stuff that gets you back to that bubbling cauldron of glee. Or, if I say it in a slightly different way, it is a reminder that you are already a superhero so you need to make a note to stop pretending to be normal.

And while I'm setting the ground rules, this book contains
no mnemonics or acronyms (well, there is one, but it's
only included as a piss-take) and I am going to endeavour
to steer clear of 'traditional' and/or tired 'olde-worlde'
theories. My view is that the world has moved on,
considerably and rapidly, and if physics has had the
quantum treatment, then so should your thinking. This is
very much a book for the 'newe worlde'.

Plus, here's some stonkingly good news: I have no plans
to make you busier than you already are. Even now you
have a to-do list that's longer than both your arms. So,
rest assured, to get maximum value from this book you
just need to read it. There isn't anything to do, as such. In
fact, often the solution to your personal awesomeness is
to do less (more of that later).

Chantal Burns puts forward the analogy that the mind
is like a magic trick. Once you have the trick explained,
it all becomes clear. There's a very high probability that
your current understanding is built on a trick of the mind.
You might want to think of this book as a cheeky glimpse
behind the curtain.

'You know, I'm not very good at magic – I can
only do half of a trick. Yes – I'm a member of
the Magic Semi-circle.'

Tim Vine

Most personal development books are about your state of
mind. The idea is that you change your habits (generally

15

towards the rosier variety) and a life of universal abundance unfolds before you. And this book has chapters that are in line with the notion that the world is neutral until you apply some thinking to it, and then it bounces off in whatever direction of spin you put on it. If you apply some positive spin to your thinking, your life will bounce off into the lush and verdant grass of positivity.

But it's not an exact science. This book is couched in the real world. You can apply as much positivity as you like but sometimes life will feel brown and gooey rather than green and lush. Yes, dear reader, the dog turd of life is out there, just waiting for you to step in it. And step in it you most certainly will. Your company press release stating the intention to move to China is not imaginary. Your granddad's demise is very real indeed. Your moody teenager really is making your life harder than it need be. And, yes, your football team has lost again. I describe these kinds of situations as being like a steaming lion turd on the top of a child's birthday cake – unpleasant in itself but also an indication of bad things to come. A bit of positive thinking might help around the edges but it's still a brown and sticky situation.

So, I promise, no bull from me.

And, finally, before we mooch off into the personal development jungle, I'd like to draw attention to one of my personal development heroes, a wonderful chap called David Taylor. I'd go so far as to say that his book The Naked Leader Experience (Bantam, 2004) changed my life. The only thing I don't like about it is the fact that David suggests you can dip in and out of his book and that he's happy for you to skip chapters and read it in any random order. No, David! You assembled the chapters in that order for a reason and I will read it in the order in which you wrote it.

Just so we're clear: I'm keen that you read all the

chapters in this book, starting at 1 and finishing at 9, in that order!

Thank you.

The dog turd of life

Chapter 2
Life intelligence

In which I introduce 'memes' and then go crazy, spotting them everywhere, from leg-warmers to fat people and peanut butter. If you have any room in the bulging suitcase of life, I suggest you pack your raincoat, even though the long-range existential forecast is 'sunny and warm'. I offer a double insult, suggesting that you are a raving 'infomaniac' as well as a 'musterbator' (no wonder you're exhausted!) and that anti-social media has led to rising irony levels where people watch box sets of *Friends*, alone.

I mention some big hitters that sound like a cross between a pop group and law firm (the Joneses, Keynes & Naish) and introduce the birth of positive thinking via a bizarre Big Bang of the God Spot and pineapple chunks.

Yes, Chapter 2 reflects life – it's bonkers.

Interesting notion
'Life is the only game in which the object of the game is to learn the rules.'
Unknown

The chase

Richard Dawkins introduced the concept of the meme, defined as 'an idea, behaviour or style that spreads from person to person within a culture', like leg-warmers suddenly, from nowhere, becoming a great idea in the 1980s. Some beliefs are called 'super-replicator memes', with the magic property of facilitating their own transmission. For example, we mimic weight. If you look around and see loads of fat people, then it seems kinda OK to join them. You're powerfully but subconsciously drawn to a fast-food joint for your lunch. The two-star assistant asks if you want it super-sizing. You eye up the people in the queue and they seem to have been super-sized so, before you know it, your fries are the extra-large variety and you're swigging from a bucket of iced Pepsi. *Burp!*

A rather fabulous example of a meme is nut allergies. I recently travelled on a proper long-haul aeroplane to the United States and there was a bing-bong over the Tannoy: 'The snack option will not be available on this flight because a passenger has a nut allergy.' Cue loads of disgruntled murmurings and suspicious looks, trying to identify the cashew-intolerant nut. Some inconsiderate passenger had robbed 350 people of their nuts in case they accidentally inhaled some dust and died. So I investigated and found that 3.3 million Americans have nut allergies. There are 2,000 hospitalizations every year and 150 deaths from food allergies, most of which are nut related. So the passenger was playing it ultra-safe, for a reason.

But, hang on, in the United States there are 45,000 deaths every year in road traffic accidents and they're not banning cars. And 13,000 gun deaths and they're most definitely not banning firearms. You end up in a bizarre situation where neighbourhoods are purged of tubs of peanut butter, but every house has a gun. Only in America, folks.

My point is that a meme is an idea that is exactly like peanut butter – it spreads. Here's another meme. Adam Smith explains that economies can blossom and grow only if people are conned into thinking that 'stuff' makes them happy. If they knew the truth, the economy would be in big trouble. In short, the pursuit of wealth does not necessarily make individuals happy but it does serve the needs of the economy that creates jobs and a stable society, thereby propagating the meme that 'buying stuff = happiness'. And we carry on as before. This is a super-replicator meme because holding it leads us to engage in the very activities that perpetuate it.

Dan Gilbert suggests the human brain's ability to plan ahead makes us 'part-time residents of tomorrow'. Something I had no idea about until I started studying was that this ability to play out future scenarios is coupled with a predisposition to rate the future as a brighter place than the present. You'd perhaps expect folk who are glum right now to imagine that things might pick up, but even people who are massively happy right now still expect their happiness to be even greater five years hence. It's a massive meme, a bit like being stuck in an existential weather forecast of 'overcast today' but 'gloriously sunny tomorrow'. This pattern of expecting the future to be brighter than today affects almost everyone so it's not a quirk, it's very much part of the human way and, of course, academics have a name for it: 'positive illusions'. Although these mental biases are incorrect (sadly, your happy tomorrow is like the real tomorrow – it never actually arrives), they serve an important evolutionary purpose.

Positive illusions entice us into believing that our strengths are more favourable than they actually are, so we stride forward in this project we call 'life'. Whether we ever get to the predicted utopian future happiness is a moot point – your positive illusion is enough to drive you forward, sniffing a wonderful carroty horizon. (This reminds me of the old joke about one snowman saying to another, 'Can you smell carrots?')

Optimism serves as a biological necessity: to keep us reproducing as a species. Basically, we believe that the next ten years will be better than this because otherwise we'd give up on our rather mundane existence. In fact, the human brain's ability to envision a better future is what differentiates us from, say, alpacas (that and their naturally water-repellent, fireproof wool).

Interesting thought
Reality: A delusional mental state caused by a pronounced deficiency of alcohol in the bloodstream.

So let me bring you back to the earlier statistic of 4,000 weeks. I don't care how old you are right now, but I promise you that you haven't got enough weeks left on this planet to be counting them down and trying to get them over with. It makes no sense whatsoever. But that thinking is ingrained in you. The mantra, insidiously seeping into you from a very early age, is that 'Mondays are bad and Fridays are good'. Oh, and Wednesdays aren't too bad because it's all downhill from there. Once that way of thinking is firmly lodged in your head, you become that person. You slouch on Mondays and skip on Fridays. But here's where it gets really spooky because nobody sat you down and taught you that Mondays are rubbish and Fridays are awesome. It's a huge societal meme, a 'wait problem' that's passed down through the generations.

It's 'groupthink' on a global scale. You end up falling into line. If you buck the trend by leaping into the office on a Monday with a hearty cry of 'Don't those weekends just drag...', then the chances are that you won't have any friends, either on Facebook or anywhere else.

I, like you, suffer from the other socially accepted meme: 'busyness'. Tony Crabbe defines the headlong rush of busyness as 'that frenetic, always alert, multi-tasking that propels us through overburdened lives. It involves always being "on", glancing regularly at our phones and jumping from task to task. It is the juggling, cramming and rushing that takes up so much of our daily existence. It is urgency, distraction and exhaustion.' And I thought, that's me! Some idiot only put 24 hours in a day and that's not nearly enough so we have to squeeze 48 hours of activity into it. It's a bit like when you've penny-pinched and only booked one bag on to your holiday flight. So, hang on a second, four people and one bag, how's that going to work? As the taxi arrives to take you to the airport, one of you is sitting on the case as the other is frantically wrestling with the zip, swimming trunks and laptop cables spilling out of the sides. Life, too, can seem as though it's bulging at the seams.

> **Symptom of busyness**
> 'I'm so busy I don't know whether I found a rope or lost my horse.'
> Mark Schaefer

And of your 24 hours, some of that has to be sleep time. So, in the bulging suitcase of life, if something's going to be left out, it's usually sleep! So now you become disturbingly busy, but with an undercurrent of sleep-deprived grumpiness.

I don't want to lay this on too thickly but 'busyness' is one of the biggest self-inflicted happiness killers. Life is turning into a massive personal time management project. Apparently, there is something called 'Hurried Woman Syndrome' (interestingly, there is no male equivalent) as well as FOBO (fear of being offline) and nomophobia (otherwise known as 'smartphone separation anxiety'). I don't need an academic paper to prove that there's been a rise in the number of people holding their phones in their hands rather than keeping them in pockets or bags. It allows quicker access, you see. In restaurants, people often have their phone on the table, breaking off conversation at every vibration. I doubt whether, among the younger generation, this is even considered rude; it's just the way it is. Gallup released figures that suggested 81 per cent of smartphone users keep their phones with them 'almost all of the time during waking hours' and 61 per cent do so even while asleep.[2] We have an attentional commitment to our mobile devices, so, even when they're not ringing or buzzing, we're still fixed on the prospect that, at any moment, they just might.

We're even trying to relax faster. I've just bought a book by Gill Farrer-Halls called *Buddhist Meditations for People on the Go* (Godsfield Press, 2005) and am learning to 'speed-meditate'. The irony of me thinking 'Excellent, cos I haven't really got time to meditate properly' has only recently sunk in. I'll do it half right. Buddhist monks will still be able to out-meditate me with one frontal lobe tied behind their backs.

Getting up close and personal, let's look at sex. I don't

know what it's like in your house but the chances are that, if you've got the time or energy at all, it has to be a quickie. And this brings me to 'multi-tasking', which makes you feel more productive but is in fact a big fat illusion – it actually makes you less productive.[3] I feel a tad squeamish linking 'sex' with 'multi-tasking' but I was once told by a conference delegate that during lovemaking she often runs through her shopping list for the following day.

As Tony Crabbe suggests, busyness is like an internal time bomb, destroying relationships from the inside.[4] It siphons attention from our loved ones. It doesn't necessarily end the relationship (although blurting out 'Don't let me forget to buy some milk' might well be a nail in your

Tony suggests busyness is like...
Internal TIME BOMB

lovemaking coffin) but it sucks all the colour and richness out.

Throughout history we've been living with scarcity and now the only scarce thing in your life is time. All this fast stuff means that we're living life beyond the legal busyness speed limit but it's important to realize that the opposite of busyness isn't slowness. As we'll see later, it's pure unadulterated attention to the moment. It's pondering, thinking, musing and wondering. These are all the things that are absent when you're speeding through life.

This next sentence takes some grappling with, so here goes: we fill every available moment with something and end up with nothing, whereas filling some moments with nothing, means you get everything.

Read it again, this time *sloooowly*. It does make sense, I promise. And now brace yourself for some controversy – I think 'busyness' and 'thin slicing' might be the easy options. Working long hours and then going home to log on to even more emails, plus cramming your electronic diary with too many appointments and not enough time, is a ruse. All this histrionic waving of hands is a whole lot easier than holding them up and saying: 'Hey, know what, something's missing.'

As Robert Holden says: 'If there's something missing in your life, it's probably you.'[5] In true time-honoured self-help tradition, it's time to find yourself.

that's a BIG one!

Tinderella -

An attractive female
discovered through the
Tinder dating application

Raving infomaniacs

You probably know what a nymphomaniac is. If not, you're probably best *not* to Google it! Let me sidestep from 'can't get enough sex' to 'can't get enough info'. Tony Crabbe describes the gush of information as 'drinking from a water fountain that has become a fire hose'. The irony of Facebook is by now known to most. The 'social' network has been linked to a surprising number of undesirable mental health consequences – depression, low self-esteem and bitter jealousy, among them.[6] I have a friend who's a head teacher and he tells me that 90 per cent of school issues boil down to social media. I'm no expert, but I think it's worth pointing out that, as social media has been on the rise, so too has loneliness. Is that a coincidence? That hints at a thousand Facebook friends equating to one real one. Get this for irony: I discovered one of my daughter's chums had stayed in and watched a box set of *Friends*, on her own!

I watched a TV programme about hoarders. These poor people were suffering from a lifetime of accumulation. Their houses were stacked from floor to ceiling with rubbish, to the point that their health and happiness were in danger. I've heard it called 'stuffocation', the process of being strangled by materialism. Just as there are mental and physical consequences of this clutter, it can be a bit like that in your head. Your home and workplace might be broadbanded, but your head isn't.

We have evolved from humans who lived in societies where not much changed, and when change did occur it was likely to be significant and perhaps life-threatening. From this background we have inherited a cognitive frailty towards novelty that throws us a modern-day conundrum: we don't like change but the modern world is awash with it.

'Keeping up with the Joneses' is a way of describing

the pernicious effect of consumerism and it afflicts us all, whether we realize it or not. As humans, we are unconsciously measuring ourselves against one another and then along came the Internet and all of a sudden there are millions of Joneses to keep up with. In today's world, it is impossible not to be reminded of how somebody, somewhere, is doing something that is much cooler than you, and be reminded of it constantly. In a bitter irony, through social media, the Internet has also open-sourced inadequacy and insecurity. I feel that consumerism has burst its banks. It's not just a steady flow, it's a riptide of social expectation and we swirl along as our teenage daughters stop eating in an effort to look like the poster-girl's airbrushed perfection.

So why don't we just stop?

J. M. Keynes reckoned that, at some point about now, humankind would have created a way of having everything it needs. And we'd flourish. I love John Naish's book *Enough: Breaking Free from the World of Excess* (Hodder, 2009) in which he argues that Keynes was half right. He was spot on about having everything we need but wrong about the bliss that would follow. His error was in not realizing that we would fail to discover the off switch to all the 'mores' of the modern world.

My work takes me all over the country and wherever I go I keep spotting examples of what must be the fastest-growing industry of the past ten years: self-storage warehousing. These cavernous businesses have mushroomed and every time I drive past one I marvel at the thinking behind it. We have accumulated so much stuff (which has failed to make us happy) that we are now renting somewhere to put it, so we can create some space at home to, you've guessed it, fill it with more stuff (which will fail to make us happy).

This glib anecdote aside, folk are often surprised at my unequivocal answer to the 'can money buy happiness' conundrum, which is a resounding YES! People wax lyrical about love, gratitude, purpose and God but I'm of the opinion that money absolutely can buy happiness. I'm a social scientist, so let me make this clear: if you plot money and happiness on a graph there is no point where money makes you sadder. However, there is a clear law of diminishing returns whereby, as income rises, it becomes harder and harder to squeeze out additional happiness.

But if we delve a bit deeper we realize that a wad of fivers and twenties is useless on its own. The marketing gurus are very good at making us unhappy. Piquing our desire for things that we didn't even know we wanted is, I have to admit, pretty darn clever. So we end up musterbating like mad. Let me clarify, 'musterbating' is when you turn things you'd like to have into things you think you absolutely *must* have. The only reason you want more money is so that you can use it to musterbate with but, even here, we've only got part of the story. Possessions are merely subsidiaries of the larger psychological objective of 'feeling great', so it's not actually the things you buy that bring you joy, it's the *feelings* you associate with them.

For example, you *think* you want some new running shoes, but you actually want the feeling of exhilaration that comes after you've been running. You *think* you want a new pair of designer jeans, but what you actually want is the warm glow of your bum looking fab in them. You *think* you want a German car, but what you actually want is a sense of satisfaction from driving it (and the psychological freedom it gives you to push into the traffic at the last minute, thus avoiding queuing like the rest of us do).

You see how it all points back to emotions?

Apologies for this sentence, but 'musterbation causes intense feelings of pleasure to wash over you'. Your new purchases will make you grin, for a short while, until habituation sets in and they lose their lustre. And you start musterbating about something else. Crikey, it's no wonder you're worn out!

But musterbation isn't exclusively a young person's thing. My father-in-law (age 82) who, for the record, drives 1.2 miles to Morrisons in Bolton twice a week using sat nav ('She keeps me company') has just signed up for the £80 offer to be upgraded to 'lifetime European road maps upgrades' despite the fact that it's a raging certainty that he's never going to go outside the borders of Lancashire. This proves that even octogenarians can still musterbate. No wonder he's nearly blind.

> ### Quote
> 'It doesn't matter how much money you've got, or how many connections, there's always something you want that's out of reach.'
> Jenson Button

In the battle to avoid stuffocating to death, here's a sentence that at first blush sounds the wrong way round:

The moment we're content, we have enough.

In fact, in terms of philosophical weight, that's probably the biggest sentence in this entire book. The problem is that our brains work the other way around. They think that when we have enough, we will be content.

Being content *first* is the key. Yes, it makes my head hurt, too!

In the Western world we now effectively have everything we could possibly need. Our cup of abundance really doth runneth over. There is no 'more' to be had. As John Naish says, we have to learn to live 'post more' and indeed that 'enoughness' is the path to contentment. In a world of enoughness the rules of the game have changed – we need a new meme – if everything is available in abundance, the challenge shifts from 'knowing where to start' to 'knowing when to stop'.

> ### A distinct possibility
> 'To be without some of the things you want is an indispensable part of happiness.'
> Bertrand Russell

But when everything is laid out before us on a never-ending table of abundance, how do we hold ourselves back? Back to the brilliant words of John Naish again: the transition from 'self-esteem' to 'us-esteem' means we have to cut out the musterbating. That's a lovely sentiment but the materialistic social comparisons arms race is a tough one to pull out of.

Those Joneses can be real bastards to keep up with.

They're just so perfect!

The God Spot

This book isn't pro or anti God but spirituality, in its widest sense, is a subject I've learned to warm to. You might be bestowed with a god to look after you. I haven't got one. (I know that if you have a god, that you think your god will look after me whether I believe or not, which is very kind of you.) Those who have a god are thankful for having him (her, it, them?) but probably also a little wary of upsetting the deity. You'd rather go to the place up above rather than down there. And the rest of us who haven't got a god are also fearful. What if we're wrong and there is one and, when we die, there really is some sort of never-ending afterlife? Perhaps we should reserve at least 1 per cent of belief, just in case?

So everyone is god-fearing in some way.

I rather like Thomas Pyszczynski's 'Terror Management Theory', in which he posits that cultural worldviews, including religious beliefs, act as a 'shield designed to control the potential for terror that results from awareness of the horrifying possibility that we humans are merely transient animals groping to survive in a meaningless universe, destined only to die and decay'. Pyszczynski rubs it in by suggesting that our lives have no more significance than a pineapple chunk. And, while you ponder that, Aleksandr Solzhenitsyn adds to your woes by pouring scorn on the Western lifestyle, arguing that we've ditched our old moral and religious frameworks, lost our sense of purpose and community, and are therefore failing to connect with life's higher meaning. There are no laughs in that.

Here's a fairly dramatic and little-known point: human brains might actually be specialized for religious experiences and have a so-called 'God Spot'. When we reflect on the immense hardship of generations gone by, it makes sense that a belief in something supernatural might help us cope. Indeed, an evolutionary perspective on religion implies that humans are inherently susceptible to religious views. The 'security blanket' concept of religion has a lot going for it. It explains why people pray during a crisis and why people living in the most miserable places on earth are almost universally religious. On the other hand, in societies that experience a good quality of life, religion loses its importance and atheism breaks out. So, although incorrectly labelled a 'God Spot' – it is neither localized as a spot, nor peculiar to experiences related to a deity – it adds a dimension to our understanding of religious experience and explains why even people in secular countries remain deeply spiritual.

This is important in that most religions offer a rather fabulous lifetime guarantee: if you can struggle through this life, there is another one of eternal abundance waiting for you. That has to be the ultimate in 'positive thinking'.

This brings me on to the question of how 'positive psychology' differs from 'positive thinking'. They're the same thing, right? Well, no, not really, but I appreciate the misunderstanding as it gives me an opportunity to get on my academic high horse.

Philosophically, positive thinking begins with the assumption that 'positive thinking is good for you'. This is often based on personal or anecdotal experience and then extrapolated to other aspects of life as a general prescription for a better life. The positive thinking movement has gathered momentum, culminating in recent years with the massive success of Rhonda Byrne's *The Secret* (Atria Books/Beyond Words, 2010), a book that prescribes tapping into the 'law of attraction' that manifests good things in your life simply by thinking about them.

Visualizing, uttering positive affirmations and having unshakable belief in the power of positivity – they work, right? Well, I guess the answer is yes and no. I'm all for positive thinking but consider the report that 20 KFC managers were injured in a firewalk. I know we shouldn't laugh at other people's misfortune but I'm pretty sure they would have had a positive pep talk and visualized success before they set off, but nursing 20 pairs of burnt feet in hospital was not such a positive outcome.

Summing it up like only he can:
'I went on a positive thinking course. It was shit.'
Gary Delaney

I am not pouring cold water on the positive thinking movement. I have trained myself to be a positive thinker and it has changed my life for the better.

But here's something bigger and better.

Positive psychology was born in the late twentieth century when Martin Seligman slapped its backside and welcomed it, kicking and screaming, as the new kid on the psychological block. That 1990s child has continued to make something of a racket. It's less like a strand of psychology and more like an ADHD teenager – it just won't sit down and shut up and I suspect it is getting more than a little annoying to some. Although I'm suggesting it was 'born' in 1995 – to stretch the metaphor beyond breaking point – you could argue that it had a gestation period longer than an elephant's.

The term was conceived by the god of management thinking, Abe 'The Hierarchy' Maslow, in the 1950s. Seligman not only borrowed it, he souped it up and the idea was formally adopted as a discrete branch of psychology. It aims to understand what is happening when individuals and organizations are working well, and build from there. The previous sentence sounds kind of obvious, but it actually turns psychology on its head. Traditionally, psychology had always been about what was wrong with you, so, for example, at university I read big thick textbooks crammed full of people with problems. That was largely because psychology was focused on fixing people and happy people didn't need fixing. It is for this precise reason that positive psychology has gained such traction. Rather than spending billions on diagnosing problems and providing horrendously expensive medical or therapeutic remedies, why not study people who are already happy? Who are they? *Why* are they? What are they doing that makes them so happy and, more to the point, what can we learn from them that we can apply to the wider population to perhaps cut depression off at the pass.

And that, as succinctly as I can put it, is the essence of the 'brave' 'new' world of positive psychology. I say 'brave' because it goes against the grain of traditional theory and some proper bona fide heavyweight psychologists still struggle to take it seriously. And I say 'new' because in subject terms it is brand-spankingly fresh. Amazingly, positive psychology still fails to appear on academic syllabuses at A level and on some psychology degree courses. Those steeped in the old ways are reluctant to embrace the problem child.

Herein lies the beauty of positive psychology – it doesn't seek to dismiss the amazing findings of 'normal psychology'; it merely looks at applying the same academic rigour to the other side of the psychology coin. Flip it, so happiness is up top. Who are the people experiencing happiness and positivity? Who are the notable few who are flourishing at work, home and in their personal relationships? Who are the people with energy and resilience? Who is it who grows rather than withers from a negative experience? You know that handful of people you can name right now (likely on the fingers of just one hand), who, when they're around, make you feel amazing ... who are they and what are they doing that makes them and you feel amazing?

Seligman posed the (now stupidly obvious) question: what can we learn from people who are flourishing, and how can we then apply what we learn across the board, giving us all room for some upwardly mobile happiness potential? Positive psychology is about conducting proper, scientifically rigorous experiments to unearth the 'secrets' (that turn out to be not too secret) of how to feel great, with the aim of spreading that knowledge for the greater good of society. That puts its moral purpose smack bang in line with its older and wrinklier ugly sister, 'normal' psychology.

I studied 'normal' psychology for years and we get on very well. We're plutonic. But once positive psychology had flashed a smile at me, it was love at first sight.

♥ ◡ ♥ Andy + Positive psychology ♥

Chapter 3
Herd intelligence

In which we take a peek at the 'why' of emotions. I mean, what's the point of them anyway? Once we get what they're all about, we move on to the 'ripple effect', and how you can make or break your friends' friends' friends' day.

What's more, if your future specs are rose-tinted, this chapter explains why your 'right now' specs have a much darker shade. It also gets to grips with why you're not oven-ready, provides a beginner's guide to your brain's dual operating system and explains why your kids look like aliens. Oh, and the chapter finishes with some magic numbers, the most important of which is #1.

Someone who just kind of 'got it'?

'The work 50 people are doing here is going to send a ripple right through the universe.'

Steve Jobs (as quoted by Walter Isaacson in the authorized biography, *Steve Jobs*)

Why we emote

Human emotions started out as a means of coordinating moods. Synchronicity of moods helped bonding, safety and teamwork. For example, a hunting party is most successful when its members are all fired up, alert and upbeat. And if one hunter senses danger, it makes sense for the others to sense it, too – not to wait for the same danger but to sense it from their own herd. Emotion is the quickest way of conveying this information. Then, at the end of the day, wild boar cooked and eaten, it would be the chief who would yawn first, everyone copied and that was the signal to go to bed, all at the same time.

So, we are conditioned to copy behaviours, but what about emotions? Emotions are feelings and they're right here, slap bang in the middle of your awareness. They are extremely variable and, in theory at least, controllable. That's because emotions aren't 'real'. By that, I mean emotions don't have a form or a shape. You can't put your emotions in a wheelbarrow and cart them around. They're a mental construct, in your head. You created them. We have four hard-wired emotional programmes that Steven Pinker calls the four Fs – feeding, fighting, fleeing and, ahem, sexual behaviour. All have primitive impulses and are basically about survival of yourself or the species.

4Fs: feeding, fighting, fleeing and, ahem, sexual behaviour

Then a new layer of brain was bolted on, right at the front. This so-called neo-cortex serves two useful purposes. First, it allows you to keep your hat on and, second, it provides some regulation to the four Fs. So a few hundred thousand years ago the human brain was upgraded with extra capacity, a bit like a new operating system. And it's this bit that raises us above, say, salmon. These fish are famous for returning to their birthplace to spawn. As they're fighting the rapids and swimming against the tide, against massive odds, leaping from bears and jagged rocks, they're not rationalizing. The salmon doesn't think 'This is just ridiculous … I'll just not bother.' It doesn't think. It just responds to its primitive instinct.

Our superior brains give us massive processing power but they are also constructed to facilitate the transfer of emotions. This puts us in line with just about every species on the planet. If you visit the Serengeti and watch a herd of impala, they will be heads down, munching on the grass, but eyes and ears alert. If one is spooked, they're all spooked. Fear transmits instantly and they're off at a pace, white tails bobbing into the distance. The transfer of emotions has saved a life and a rumbling tum means that the lion doesn't sleep tonight.

In my training courses, I use the phrase 'everything speaks' – what you say and how you say it is important but your 'message' is much bigger than that. Your clothes are telling a story. Your body language is screaming a message. Your face is a dead giveaway. Your house décor is whispering subtly. And the story they are telling is 'this is who I am and what I stand for'.

The biggest message you send is via your emotions, so let's experiment with a couple of them and see how they manifest as 'communication'. Facial expressions are there for a reason, most notably to warn others. Nowadays, you get the milk out of the fridge and give it a quick sniff just to make sure. If it's humming, 'disgust' involves a wrinkling of the nose that closes the nostrils and you recoil to avoid the stench. Chances are, in today's relatively hygienic world, the worst thing you will experience is eating a rasher of bacon that is slightly green at the edges. But back in the campfire days, before fridges were invented, you'd kill a boar and have nowhere to keep it refrigerated, so you'd eat what you could and then sit the carcass in the shade of a tree, powerless to stop the buzzing flies from laying their eggs on your next meal. Your ancestors ate a lot of rotten food! And if it was too far gone, it'd give them a very upset tummy or maybe even kill them. So a good sniff before you tucked into the maggot-infested boar was a good idea. The wrinkling of the nose and a hefty 'ugh!' served as a warning to the tribe that this food was very off indeed. You felt disgusted and communicated it to others for the greater social good.

Anger is another interesting emotional case study. *Toy Story*'s Mr. Potato Head has a face for every occasion, so do me a favour and pull your angry face. I know you were trying out your disgusted face a few seconds ago just to check that it did indeed close your nostrils. So now I'm daring you to do 'anger', even if you're reading this on the train. Go on, just for a second. And let me guess. You snarled, bared your teeth and, if you did the full-body version, you will actually have transformed your fingers into claws. And you did this for a reason. You are communicating to those around you that you're not for messing with. *Back off, buddy! Check out these gnashers – they're sharp. And these fingernails can make one helluva scratch.*

Anger and its close cousin rage are classic examples of emotions that are deemed bad but are actually very useful. We get angry for a reason. In the olden days you'd see an enemy burning your house down and rage would kick in, giving you near-superhuman powers to fight them off. Fast forward to today and we still have the same basic emotional circuitry. So now a traffic warden gives you a ticket and you want to kill him. Mostly, we bottle it and avoid physical harm, although sometimes it's quite an internal battle. Perhaps just baring your teeth and doing the claws thing at them would suffice?

On an incredibly serious note, there was a recent tragic event reported on the news, a truly awful situation involving an armed man on the loose. He was shooting indiscriminately. There were no eyewitnesses because they were all dead so the reporter interviewed a guy who didn't actually see the incident but this is what he said: 'I saw a man running away. His face told me something awful was happening, so I ran too.'

So, although emotions happen internally, they have a habit of spilling out into the external world. They are nature's way of equipping us for survival. All emotions, even negative ones, have positive intent.

Interesting thought

'Fear is useful. It stops us doing stupid things. Without fear we would have tigers as pets and we would juggle chainsaws for giggles. That might not work out well for some.'

Chris Baréz-Brown

The ripple effect

Emotional contagion works on the outside and the inside. We are biologically driven to mimic others outwardly and, in mimicking their outward displays, we also end up adopting their inner states. At its simplest level, someone smiles because they feel happy – you mimic the smile and also feel happy. So, far from other people not being able to make us feel anything, we are in fact hard-wired in ways that predispose us to feel their joy and pain. If my football team is on a bad run it has an impact on the whole of Derby, just like Manchester United on a bad run creates an emotional stampede that depresses the whole of the south of England. (Yes, that's a footballing gag. For non-football fans, I'm not going to explain it because explaining a joke is like dissecting a frog. You understand it better but the frog dies in the process.)

Happiness seeds

Plant them

While it's true that we cannot force people to be positive, we can plant seeds. It is truly a case of leading by example. Your attitudes and behaviours are infectious. I guess the million-dollar question is: will people benefit from what they catch? Your emotions are bigger than you. In *Connected: The Amazing Power of Social Networks and How They Shape Our Lives* (Little, Brown, 2009), Nicholas Christakis and James Fowler make the point beautifully, describing the complex web of social connections thus: 'Ties do not extend outward in straight lines like spokes on a wheel [...] Instead

hyper-dyadic spread?

these paths double back on themselves and spiral around like a tangled pile of spaghetti.' They call it the 'hyper-dyadic spread' – the tendency of emotions to spread from person to person, beyond an individual's direct social ties. Indeed, there is evidence to suggest that your emotions have a ripple effect that reaches three degrees of people removed from you. You are therefore affecting you friends' friends' friends. So, if you've got a smile and a positive attitude, everyone with whom you come into direct contact experiences an emotional uplift of 16 per-cent. So, that's terrific news because you're raising the emotional tone of your family, friends and work colleagues. But it doesn't stop there. Those 16-per-cent-happier folk then pass on their happiness to everyone they encounter, raising their levels by 10 per cent. Remember, you haven't actually met these ten-percenters directly, but they have caught your happiness. And, to complete the ripple, these 10-per-cent-happier folk pass your happiness on to everyone they meet by another 6 per cent.

Let me boil this down to what it means to me, every single day. If I get out of bed and choose to be my best self (remember that's a conscious choice and, at 6 a.m., an effort) then at 7 a.m., when my teenagers venture downstairs for breakfast, I am more likely to be beaming and chatty while I serve their Cheerios. So, the ripple effect suggests that my teenagers should now be 16 per cent happier simply because I'm in the room. That's terrific value, and all by 7 a.m.

I'm first to leave the house, driving to wherever work takes me. My kids will walk to the bus stop and await their transport. As the bus pulls up, the odds are stacked in favour of my 16-per-cent-happier teenagers actually smiling at the driver and bidding her a good day. The bus driver is smiling as she drives to school – 10 per cent happier – thinking that the newspapers have got it wrong and young people nowadays seem very happy and polite. The bus driver drops the kids off and returns to the depot where she has a cup of tea with the other bus drivers. The ripple effect means that the other bus drivers are now 6 per cent happier and, the very best bit, I haven't even met the bus driver or been to the depot. How cool is that? If I can create happiness that ripples across my home town.

And that's me, one person, making a positive attitudinal choice at 6 a.m. How many people do you come into direct contact with every single day, raising their levels by 16 per cent? How many of those people 'infect' your workplace by 10 per cent. And how many of those go home and infect their families by 6 per cent?

Let me do the sums for you: at a conservative estimate, let's assume you meet 3 people at home, 15 work colleagues, 3 people in the supermarket queue, a shop assistant, the lady behind the counter at the petrol station, plus you smile at 5 random strangers – that's 28 people that you've come into direct contact with. For the sake of simplicity, let's assume that they also meet 28 people and those 28 also meet 28. Your happiness therefore ripples to 21,952 people. And that's a conservative estimate! If you're in a 'people job' such as teaching or nursing, you are meeting many more than 28 people so your sphere of influence is jaw-dropping. Plus, if your entire team is aware of the ripple effect, you are spreading good emotions across the workplace and your community in a mini-tsunami of positivity.

So, all's rosy in the garden. You are literally an inspiration to your friends, your friends' friends and your friends' friends' friends. On a good day, that is. But as we know, not every day is a good day, so it's worth examining the other side of the emotional coin.

The evolution of negative

Scary thought
The only difference between a rut and a grave is the depth of the hole.

We enter this world naked in every respect – firstly in the stark-bollock way but also in that we are a blank canvas. A clean slate, if you like. Babies have no mask or persona. They're not pretending to be themselves or indeed anyone else. They have what Zen Buddhists call the 'original face'. They aren't trying to fit in. Babies are less like 'human beings' and more 'humans being'.

> Interesting thought
> 'We were all born naked, the rest, is all DRAG.'
> Jackie Huba

But it's not long before the blank canvas gets scrawled on and the learned self begins to take over.

Brace yourself for a weird contradiction. I spent the previous chapter suggesting that we are driven forwards by 'positive illusions', which are essentially a collection of happiness mirages that stop us throwing the towel in. The inference was that we have a strong optimistic sat nav. Indeed, my own research shows that almost everyone has the belief that the future will be much better than the past and present. We keep peering into the distance through our 'finer future goggles' because they protect and inspire us, inching us forward rather than to the nearest high-rise ledge.

But hang on, if optimism is built into our system, how is it that the voice in your head is so negative? This is another of those technical points that will only be of interest to the purist but I'll explain it anyway. It seems that optimism is reserved for your 'future goggles' so you're scanning the horizon through a rose-tinted glow.

Sadly, your 'now goggles' don't have the same pink hue. They are tinged with realism and everything can seem stark, scary and negative. Negativity bias means that we tend to have a critical voice in our head that judges ourselves and other people and notices negatives in the here and now. So why has evolution equipped us to see happiness on the horizon but negativity now?

This is perhaps an example that benefits from looking through the opposite end of the kaleidoscope. Imagine, just for a second, that human minds were constructed the other way around, to be 'very happy now' and 'much less happy in the future'? We might well be enjoying the moment but would be scared stiff of moving forwards. We'd stop striving and civilization would grind to a halt. Our ultra-happy ancestors might never have ventured far from their tribes and we might all be cave dwellers, still huddled together and dreaming of light and heat.

The more you think about it, the more feelings of caution, negativity and quiet discontent *now* make perfect sense. The reason we're tuned into negative is that positives are less pressing. As Jon Haidt reminds us, we have been sharing this planet with all sorts of creatures that can eat, sting, bite and even electrocute us for the best part of 200,000 years. The only thing that has changed in the past few hundred years is us: large-scale deforestation and expanding urbanization have wiped out or marginalized entire species that previously posed a danger to our existence.

Richard Dawkins's 'selfish gene' reveals that we are programmed for self-survival. Therefore, being hyper-vigilant for danger was a good thing, or at least back in the day of eaty, bitey, stingy, electrocutey beasties. If you missed a rustle of the grass, there were no second chances – you were a gonner – whereas if you miss a happiness opportunity, you will get another.

Because survival is your brain's number-one objective, it goes to the trouble of storing negative memories (bad people, awful smells, terrible experiences, embarrassing incidents, dangerous animals, et al.) in an easy-to-reach place for future reference. In the equivalent of your garage storage system, happy, joyful memories are collecting dust at the back while panic, negativity and fearful memories are totally accessible, right there by the door.

The problem is that this negativity is so in-your-face forceful that it can become overpowering. Every time you open your mind's garage door, wham, it's right there. Negativity can become the norm, easily accessed, bringing you to your knees with panic attacks and depression.

Bigger than average!

Big heads

Dolphins are born swimming. Turtles are born with an instinct to run to the sea as fast as their flippers will take them. If you watch veterinary programmes where a calf is born, the mum gives it a bit of a lick clean and it's on its wobbly legs within an hour. Most animals are born world-ready.

World ready

We are not 'most animals'. Humans are unique in so many cranial ways, not least in that compared to other primates our babies are born too early for their brains to be fully developed. We'd need to gestate for two years if we were to emerge fully brained. We pop out at nine months because our heads won't fit through that tiny escape hatch. If we stayed in there any longer, single children would be the norm and our mums would probably never walk again.

Alien Baby

So, head-size is a problem that evolution has solved by birthing our offspring before they're properly ready. Your brain was disproportionately large compared to other organs when you were born – that's why babies look a bit like aliens (not yours, of course – yours are cute – just other people's babies). The result of coming out of the oven before we're properly baked means that human babies are totally helpless. (Speaking as a dad of two teenagers, some stay that way until they're 24.) Jon Haidt suggests that this is why we're programmed to love our children. If we give birth to helpless offspring, we have to feel love in order to want to nurture them.

Dan Kahneman suggests our ancient brain was constructed according to the needs at that time. He calls it 'system 1', the ultra-quick, instinctive part of your brain. Its job is not to think, merely react. In fact, system 1 acts faster than you can think. Put your hand on a hotplate and you'll see what I mean – there's no 'Mmm, what's that burning smell?'; system 1 acts at supersonic speed.

Top tip

Conventional wisdom suggests that if you're angry you should 'count to 10', which allows the red mist to evaporate.

Research suggests that once the source of anger is removed your emotion system returns to normal after about 20 minutes. So, here's a top emotional intelligence tip: don't count to 10 when you're mad, count to 1,200!

Then, about ten thousand years ago, the human brain experienced a growth spurt and along came the limbic system, which is all about nurturing and emotion. Then another spurt and we got the pre-frontal cortex, the executive brain that, on a good day, gives self-control, thinking, imagining, planning, reviewing, communicating and moralizing. Kahneman calls this somewhat slower function 'system 2' and most of the time it engages in what's called 'confirmation bias', just tagging along, agreeing with system 1. It's easier to rubber-stamp your autopilot responses so we tend to do the same thinking, have the same prejudices and come to the same conclusions.

That's why, as adults, we tend to be stuck with ourselves, entombed in a lifetime of learned habits, thinking and behaviours.

Important numbers

7 – The number of deadly sins but also the world's favourite lucky number

42 – The meaning of life (according to *The Hitchhiker's Guide to the Galaxy*)

3 – The magic number according to De La Soul's 1990 hit record. Also, a crowd

57 million – The number of anti-depressants prescribed in England per annum

4,000 – The number of weeks in the average UK lifespan

One-seventh – The fraction of your life that is spent on Mondays. Too many to wish away

2.9013 – The so-called 'Losada-line', the positive to negative ratio you need to maintain a relationship

150 – According to UK anthropologist Robin Dunbar, this is the maximum size for a social grouping to have a feeling of cohesion. Neolithic villages, apes, army units are all organized in groups of around 150

15 – Tim Kasser reckons that there are 15 people who form the core of your life. These relationships will nourish and sustain you. So overinvest your time in the 15. You can be a failure on social media but hugely happy if you have a close-knit 15

7 – Yes, again! The number of seconds it takes for love to transfer in a hug

#1 – Someone you really should look after

Chapter 4
Research intelligence

A hilarious chapter that starts with entrails and ends with a brain tumour. OK, not so funny, but sandwiched in between is a healthy filling of emotional intelligence as well as the question: who's cleverer, your esteemed Ph.D.'d author or his totally thick mate from school?

After discovering that the rather perplexing answer is 'both', this chapter explores some academic big-hitters (Dan Goleman and Howard Gardiner) and looks at the fragility of positive emotions before explaining why we need to strengthen them.

After a quick trip to Japan we have time to look at lots of happy things like marshmallows, unicorns and cheese string. I introduce a new word – *hygge* – look at a Yorkshire fridge full of flu virus before jumping aboard the mindfulness bandwagon, I have to say, with a degree of gay (old definition) abandon.

How it works
'Evidence is not enough. I want to be emotionally persuaded.'

Unknown

Strapping you in

I'm not sure that anecdotes can be 'gory but cute', but here goes. When I was about five our cat proudly delivered a freshly killed mouse to the kitchen. Thomas (she was actually a girl cat but let's gloss over that) sat proudly, licking the entrails off her paws. The mouse was a gonner for sure. Its tummy had been expertly slit and some of its insides were hanging out. I squatted to examine this new information. 'Hey, Mummy,' I remember saying, 'I can see its feelings hanging out.'

I'm not entirely sure why I would confuse its liver and kidneys with 'feelings'? The only thing I can think is that, even at five, I knew 'feelings' were inside you. And as I sit here tapping away at this chapter, I'm discovering that, back in 1971, I wasn't a million miles away from the truth.

So thank goodness for skin. Imagine what we'd be without it. You are a vessel of various juices, chemicals, bones and slimy stuff, sluicing about. Take the skin away and you'd be a dollop of warm entrails. I could rummage around in the mess, but I'd not be able to find your 'feelings'.

So these 'feelings', where the hell are they? And what are they? Well, to find your feelings I'd have to collect a beaker of your juices and put them through some laboratory tests where we'd find you are also a Molotov cocktail of chemicals. Dan Goleman uses a nice turn of phrase: 'the brain's wetware is awash in a messy, pulsating puddle of neurochemicals'.[7] You are the dealer of these chemicals; you're also the manufacturer.

TOP TIP:

Don't judge people by their outward appearance. Study their entrails.

#ArdaghTips

So how do you decide which chemicals to deal in? *Thoughts*, that's how. The idea is that I whet your appetite with some snippets of big stuff that I'll come back to later. If we're going to shoot you into the enlightenment stratosphere, I need to get you strapped in and comfortable with some of the basics first. I don't want you getting up there and not being able to breathe!

So let's start this chapter with a biggie. If you look at happy and not-so-happy people, they're the same flesh-and-blood creatures with the same experiences, brains, weather, jobs and pressures. We can argue about genetic make-up and, of course, you can be born with a greater probability of being happy, but the here-and-now differences lie squarely in your circumstances and thinking.

Which is correct?

'Either this life I'm in is very dream-like, or this dream I'm in is very life-like.'

Ashleigh Brilliant

Remember from earlier how I suggested that your reality isn't real? Yes, I know you're still smarting from that one, but it will become clear by the end of Chapter 7, I promise! For now, let me regale you with a study by Ellen Langer that shows the interplay between circumstances and thinking. She recruited a group of men in their 80s for a weekend of reminiscences and nostalgia. She organized a themed event that took them back 30 years, creating a retreat that had no old-age props such as walking frames or handrails. Instead, they were immersed in the music, brands and TV of 30 years ago and lived as though they were 50 years old.

'Before' and 'after' tests showed significant improvements in blood pressure, memory, eyesight and hearing. This begins to show the relationship between thought, self-perception and behaviour. By changing the external environment, she managed to change their thinking, and by changing their thinking they produced different emotions, which changed their reality. Forgive me for hammering this one but the men's years fell away to the point that there were changes in their physiology and improvements in their health – in one weekend!

I ask you, how powerful is that?

H-spot

We've looked briefly at the God Spot. There is, apparently, something called a G-spot that is somewhat different – under no circumstances should you ever get them confused! ('We got a dog last Christmas and called him G-spot. I can't find him anywhere.')

↓ EFGHIJK

So having used up my one and only G-spot gag, I'll inch along the alphabet and invent the H-spot. Here's how it works: if you go with acknowledged wisdom and believe that the problem is 'out there', you will always be trying to change your job, house, partner, looks or car – searching for the centre of that Venn diagram where everything intersects perfectly. That tiny intersection of 'perfect everything' is where you'll find your happiness – your 'H-spot' – you'll know it when you find it. And, crikey, it can be harder to find than your G-spot!

Despite the innuendos, there's a big concept on the way and it's another of those points that I'm going to drop in and leave well alone for now, returning to it in a later chapter. So here goes: most personal development is about 'changing your thinking', a concept that I don't disagree with. But we get stuck at the level of learning about swapping one thought for another – usually a negative gets the heave-ho and is replaced by a positive. This is the basis for a lot of talking-based therapies, such as cognitive behavioural therapy (CBT).

This can be very useful, but essentially you end up swapping the content rather than the process. As Richard Wilkins thought-provokingly puts it, you don't change the tide by standing in the sea. So, if someone's upsetting you, you can change your thinking, create different stories and reframe as much as you like, but that other person still has the power to piss you off. You change the tide by going to the Moon. Understanding the nature of thought (how thought works) shifts your moon and gets you a much more interesting result. This has the power to generate a spontaneous shift of consciousness that allows you to see life from a more objective vantage point. The view from 'up here' is more panoramic than the one 'down there', so there's less need for 'positive thinking'. It's all just 'thinking'. Everything you experience is just thought.

Yes, you might have to re-read that paragraph several times and, no, it probably still won't make a whole lot of sense. Which is why I said I'd drop it in and scuttle off to more well-trodden territory, safe in the knowledge that it's in your subconscious so it'll be easier to grasp when I come back to it later on.

you might need to re-read this one!

Emotional intelligence

This one is in the book title, so it needs a space all of its own. Let's start with a couple of technical points to clear them out of the way, hopefully giving us a clear run.

There's a bit of hoo-hah about who first coined the term 'emotional intelligence'? The general debate seems to be a three-way tug-of-war between some of the names that crop up in this section – Peter Salovey &John Mayer, Goleman and Gardner. However, I don't want to burst anyone's bubble but in *The Nicomachean Ethics* Aristotle postulated that, in order to achieve what he called 'the good life', it was necessary to manage our emotional life with intelligence. And that was written 300 years before baby Jesus was born. So I'm not going to muddy myself in whether emotional intelligence is a new subject or who got there first. The point is that we're here, now, and we need to know what it means, whether it matters and, if it does, what we can do about it.

Salovey & Mayer's modern concept of emotional intelligence has morphed into a mishmash of ideas. The best starting point is probably the thorny question: 'How "clever" are you?' You're reading this book so, hey, you can probably afford a slightly smug inward nod to yourself – it may have pictures but this ain't no comic book.

Tracking back, it was Howard Gardner's *Frames of Mind: The Theory of Multiple Intelligences* (Basic Books, 1983) that gave an influential nudge of the first domino that began to topple the meme that IQ was the be-all and end-all of intelligence. Here's an example. One of my best buddies, Pat, left school with no qualifications whatsoever. Zilch! I mean, after 15 years of schooling, leaving empty-handed is pretty much an achievement in its own right. But my not-so-bright mate is now a fantastic dad who also runs a successful building company and he can build houses, fit kitchens, plaster walls, lay patios and tile roofs. Meanwhile I went on to get a Ph.D. so must be 'proper clever', right? Err, wrong. If you ask me to put a shelf up, I guarantee it won't stay up very long. And as for building a house or fitting a kitchen...

So, which of us is the cleverer? Gardner's rather neat

answer is both of us. He asserts that there are at least seven intelligences, only two of which – verbal and mathematical – are academic. Into the mix he tossed spatial (as used by artists or architects), kinaesthetic (found in sportspeople), musical (found in Mozart and probably not hip-hop artists) and a couple of 'personal intelligences' – interpersonal and intrapersonal.

It is the combination of these so-called 'multiple intelligences' that makes up your all-round cleverness. Gardner, to his credit, said this was the starting point and that there was no magic number, ironically getting a bit too clever and stretching things to a bewildering 20 intelligences.

But it's these last two 'personal intelligences' that are of particular interest for this book. Gardner summarizes them as follows:

'Interpersonal intelligence is the ability to understand other people: what motivates them, how they work, how to work cooperatively with them.' Or, stated in a slightly different way: 'Capacities to discern and respond appropriately to the moods, temperaments, motivations and desires of other people.'

Intrapersonal intelligence is subtly but importantly different, defined as '... a correlative ability, turned inward. It is a capacity to form an accurate model of oneself and to be able to use that model to operate effectively in life' or, with a slightly different spin, 'access to one's own feelings and the ability to discriminate among them and draw upon them to guide behaviour'.

You instinctively know when someone is attuned to you. In psychological terms, you 'feel felt' and you develop a high-quality relationship that the emotional intelligence literature would call 'rapport'. As a quick rapport gauge, think of someone in your life with whom you get on like a house on fire or the handful of people that, five minutes after you met, you felt like you'd known for ever.

Contrast with folk you've known for a long time but with whom you feel awkward. Maybe someone at work you wouldn't want to share a elevator with because you wouldn't know what to say. That journey from the ground floor to the fifth seems like for ever as you stare at the floor, struggling to converse.

Now this isn't an exact science but, as a rough guide, you are in rapport with the 'getting on like a house on fire' person and out of rapport with the 'longest ascent to the fifth floor' person.

The award-winning, eminent guru Dr Daniel Goleman proposed five 'domains' of what he terms EQ ('emotional quotient'):

Goleman's original concept had five 'domains':

1. Knowing your emotions.

2. Managing your own emotions.

3. Motivating yourself.

4. Recognizing and understanding other people's emotions.

5. Managing relationships.

The first three of these relate to *personal* competence – self-awareness, self-regulation and self-motivation. The starting point is always yourself. Think about it: until you stop and identify your emotions – 'What am I feeling and where did the feeling come from?' – you cannot master them. The remaining two pertain to *social* competence –

social awareness and social skills.

It's curious that first time around I really struggled with Goleman's book. It has the words 'Number 1 bestseller' emblazoned on the cover and I remember getting to page 17 and giving up. I imagined that either people were a lot cleverer than me or it was a coffee-table book, left lying around the house, unread, to merely make you look intelligent. And now I love it, especially because Goleman translates the cumbersome 'metacognition' and 'metamood' into the nice and simple 'self-awareness'. And it is this quality of self-awareness that is the starting point for emotional intelligence. But don't read too much into it because, as Goleman states, 'self-awareness is not an attention that gets carried away by emotions [...] rather it is neutral mode that maintains self-reflectiveness even amidst turbulent emotions'.[8] It seems that self-awareness is a slight stepping back from experience so you are aware of what is happening but not lost in it. It's the difference between flipping your lid at your teenager coming home later than they promised, and thinking: 'This is anger I'm feeling. How can I best move forward?' In this second scenario, you are more in control of your emotions and therefore, the thinking goes, better likely to craft a positive outcome. (Please note that, on occasion, flipping your lid at your teenager is appropriate, just not all the time.)

So, next up, are some emotions better than others? That's easy – yes and no! All emotions are, in essence, a call to action. They represent an impulse to do something or, to use Paul McKenna's analogy, a knock on the door. The word 'emotion' is derived from the Latin *motere*, 'to move', so an emotion creates motion and all emotions have positive intent. Fear sends blood to your legs so you can fun further and faster than you've ever run before. Love, and especially sexual satisfaction, creates the opposite of fight or flight. Men, in particular, experience a flow of calmness and contentment akin to a nest-building instinct. This state of 'parasympathetic arousal' means that men want to have a hug and then go to sleep. So, top tip: in the aftermath of lovemaking, your man will agree to anything, so long as you let him snooze.

Happiness is an interesting emotion. Whereas fight-or-flight emotions close your thinking down, happiness opens the mind up to possibilities and creative solutions about how to move forward.[9]

It's a strange admission for a happiness expert but personally I am not overly keen on organized happiness. Karaoke makes me shudder and party games bring me out in a cold sweat. However, while I have reservations about 'planned happiness', I take the subject of happiness very seriously indeed. So hang fire before you blurt out that it's not a 'proper subject' or a 'real thing'. My wrath will be incurred, thereby making me upset and illustrating the first rule of happiness – it can be very fragile indeed.

It may be brittle, but happiness is a very big deal. It's the thing that you want more of, and in a global survey it easily topped the list of what you want for your children and grandchildren.[10]

Here's something you already know – happiness is good for you. As well as helping you look even more gorgeous, smiling reduces stress, lowers blood pressure and enhances other people's perceptions of whoever is wearing the smile.[11] But happiness is much more than just a pretty face. There is a plethora of evidence suggesting that happiness can influence health in positive ways, most notably improving your lifespan.[12] People who feel positive in their lives 'grow psychologically' as well as becoming more optimistic, resilient, open, accepting

TOP TIP:

happiness makes you look even more gorgeous

and purposeful.[13] In addition, happiness builds social connections and is energizing and contagious.[14]

Happiness sends out more of the chemical dopamine[15] and opioids,[16] and there is evidence that happiness will also reduce the propensity for a number of other ailments: lower blood pressure,[17] less pain[18] and less likelihood of diabetes and stroke,[19] plus happy people sleep better.[20]

Marshmallows and unicorns – the shifting sands of happiness

In Okinawa, Japan, they have a lovely word, *ikagai* (pronounced 'itchy-guy'), which is defined as the reason you get up in the morning. Your *ikagai* is your purpose and, once fuelled, it drives your internal engine. Therefore the chances are that all great people are just ordinary people with a strong itchy-guy.

We seem to have been seeking purpose or the meaning of life for pretty much as long as there has been life. And while I've no idea what the meaning of life is or, indeed, whether we're supposed to be pondering why we're here, the truth, as Tim Minchin so eloquently put it, is that life is long, tough and tiring. It can be a pretty empty existence so you may as well try to fill it with compassion, love, enthusiasm and happiness.

What's the point in doing anything other?

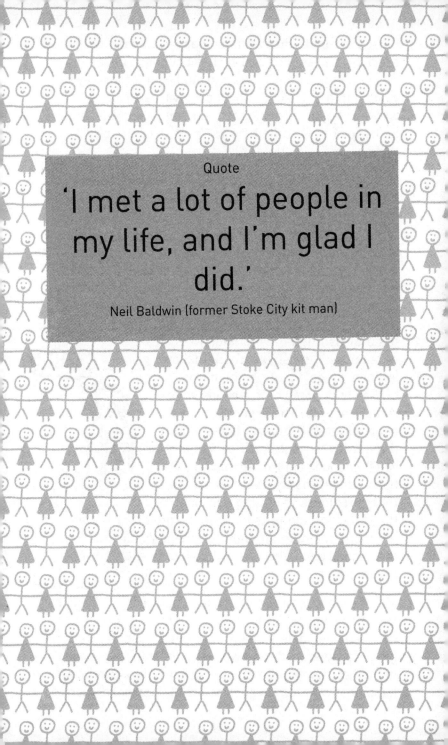

Quote

'I met a lot of people in my life, and I'm glad I did.'

Neil Baldwin (former Stoke City kit man)

What's the difference between happy and positive? There are a lot of Facebook and Twitter postings suggesting 'happiness is a choice'. Having studied it for donkey's years, I'm not so sure. I think positivity is a choice whereas happiness is something that you have to allow. So happiness is something you have to open up to. I think...

As science hardens and our belief in heaven softens, there is a trend away from the postponement of happiness to some point in the future, towards a quest for immediate satisfaction. It's like Stanford University's famous marshmallow experiment, but on a lifetime scale. In case you don't know, Walter Mischel took a bunch of small children and offered them a choice – they could either have one marshmallow now or, if they waited 15 minutes, they could have two. After explaining the rules, the professor left the room for 15 minutes with the single marshmallow left behind, on a plate, right in front of the child. Some of these kids were three years old! The experiment has been repeated dozens of times, and if you trawl through YouTube footage you'll find kids squirming, hiding behind their fingers, even licking the marshmallow and putting it back on the plate. For some, as soon as the professor leaves the room, the marshmallow is gone, down in one. Sod the second one – this one will do just fine. It's a proper chuckle-fest.

Mischel's academic point is one of delayed gratification. He followed up with the children and found that those who had been able to delay their gratification scored higher academically and were still better able to resist immediate temptation. So, the ability to forego a bit of happiness now for a bigger dollop of happiness later on might be one of the crucial points to achieving long-term happiness. I would imagine that you can correlate those who resist the marshmallow with those who save for a pension and those who scoff it as spending every penny as soon as they get it.

Happiness, like other emotions, is not something you obtain but rather something you inhabit. What this implies is that happiness is not achieved in itself, but rather it is the side effect of a particular set of on-going life experiences. When most people seek happiness, they are actually seeking pleasure: good food, more sex, more time for TV and movies, a new car, parties with friends, full body massages, losing ten pounds, becoming more popular, and so on.

But while pleasure is great, it's not the same as happiness. Pleasure is correlated with happiness, but does not cause it. Ask any drug addict how their pursuit of pleasure turned out. Ask a 30-stone man who has almost eaten himself to death how pursuing instant pleasure has made him feel in the long term.

It's also very important to realize that happiness isn't a fixed thing. It matures as you do. When you're young, you dream of things that will make you happy. I remember being allowed to stay up until midnight on New Year's Eve when I was ten. I was giddy about staying up all night and never ever sleeping again. I eventually conked out on the sofa at 11.58 p.m. *Doh!* When you're little, everything is new and exciting. You dream of sliding down the world's biggest slide and bouncing on the bounciest

#Dreams of the young
forevs

trampoline that will jettison you into the clouds, where you might sit awhile sucking lollipops and guzzling chocolate fizzy-ade. And you'll have a pet unicorn (rainbow-coloured, obviously) and you'll exist on birthday cake and cheese string. Like for forevs!

And then you get older and 'happiness' morphs into something more akin to 'contentment'. All of the things above make you shudder. Staying up all night? Crikey, how awful! The best thing ever is being tucked up, snuggly and warm, nice and early. The thought of big slides and trampolines is enough to make your stomach churn, that unicorn would just shit everywhere and the house would be a nightmare to keep clean. As for fizzy drinks, you'd rather have a nice cup of tea. Oh, and cheese string makes you vomit.

It's rather like a computer game, where life has various happiness levels. You complete a particular level, say, 'unicorns and lollipops' at age six, and progress to the seven-to-eleven level 'holding hands and school trips' happiness level. Your final level might be, say, 'snoozing in front of an old movie on a Saturday afternoon'. I think it's safe to say that the extremes are gradually evened out as you progress through the levels and that 'happiness' morphs from the energetic 'arriving at the beach, tearing your clothes off and sprinting to the sea' that characterizes childhood, to a more sedate 'arriving at the beach and smiling as your grandkids sprint to the sea'. You can't trade one off against the other or argue that one contains more happiness than the other – they're both equally valid forms of 'happiness' – they are just manifested differently.

If you're like me, and you find that your life has become more about pursuing peace and relaxation than giddy excitement, rest assured that you aren't missing out on happiness. Your happiness has evolved, just as you have. Even though our version seems less fun by the standards of our younger selves, that doesn't mean it's less good.

There's a Danish word, *hygge*, that I think we need to adopt. Pronounced 'hoo-ga', it has no direct English translation. Sitting by the fire on a cold night, wearing a woolly jumper, while drinking hot chocolate and stroking the cat on my knee – that's pretty much *hygge*. Eating home-made cake, being wrapped up in scarf and beanie on an early-morning walk, Earl Grey served in a proper china cup, family get-togethers at your mum's, getting into a bed warmed through by an electric blanket – they're all *hygge*, too.

The best approximation is 'cosiness' but it's much more than that. *Hygge* is an entire attitude to life that helps Denmark to consistently rank in the world's top three happiest countries.

In her book *The Year of Living Danishly* [Icon Books Ltd, 2015], Helen Russell suggests that: 'The rest of the world seems to be slowly waking up to what Danes have been wise to for generations – that having a relaxed, cosy time with friends and family, often with coffee, cake or beer, can be good for the soul.' This simple statement is more important than it might seem. It mentions family and friends and hints at what we already know – that relationships are crucial to happiness. Eating cake and drinking beer on your own might be very tasty but it's certainly not *hygge*. A sense of belonging is crucial, whether that's to a family or community. And this is where there is massive strain on happiness in the UK. We are so busy that we don't know who lives next door, or our family members are so dispersed that we get to see them only once in a blue moon. Social media have opened up the communication channels so that you can be in touch with anyone – via a keyboard – but that's most certainly not *hygge*.

List all the people whose funeral you would go to if they died this week.

Activity part 2

Spend time with the people on your list.

Just visiting or moving in?

People talk of happiness as a journey rather than a destination and I get that, but I think it's a destination, too. I'd rather live *in* Happy Town than on the outskirts peeping in, or just visiting on my holidays.

So, if you throw everything into the mix, emotional intelligence is the ability to make healthy choices based on accurately identifying, understanding and managing your own feelings and those of others. And are some emotions better than others? Well, frankly, happiness and positivity have a lot of benefits, so it would seem appropriate to steer yourself towards these if you possibly can. Healthy emotional functioning is the starting point for everything else falling into line. Here's some proper research, and I know it's proper because it's from Yorkshire where, apparently, they have a fridge full of the flu virus. If you take someone who is emotionally upbeat and expose them to said fridge, 27 per cent will come down with flu. Those who are already stressed or feeling a bit low stand a 47 per cent chance of getting the bug.[21] And, obviously, the male version of said flu is so much worse.

'Happiness doesn't flow from success; it actually causes it.'

Professor Richard Wiseman

If we ratchet the illness up to a heart attack, pessimists have much less chance of being alive eight years later than their optimistic counterparts, with Chris Peterson and his colleagues suggesting that optimism is a bigger factor than any medical risk factor.[22] In terms of been-there-done-that, it's hard to argue with Holocaust survivor Victor Frankl's conclusion that hope is the differentiator when the going gets *beyond* tough.

But, despite researching happiness for the best part of ten years, I do not subscribe to the 'always be happy' ideology. Denying sad feelings leads to deeper and more prolonged negative emotions and emotional dysfunction. Excuse the lack of academic language here but the simple reality is that shit happens, or, put another way, just when you think all is lost, you lose something else. Things go wrong. People upset us. Mistakes are made and negative emotions arise. And that's fine.

Shit happens!

Interesting thought from someone who should know
'Everyone has a plan until they're punched in the face.'
Mike Tyson

You cannot control what another person is thinking or feeling, but you can master your side of the equation. And, if you get it right, you may not control other people but you will surely influence them. Emotional intelligence isn't about squelching bad feelings. Nor is it about running from them or pretending they don't exist. The trick with negative emotions is to express them in a socially acceptable and healthy manner and in a way that aligns with your values. Emotional intelligence tends to always lead me back to square one, the *appropriateness* of an emotion and your ability to stay as upbeat as possible while accepting the inevitability of some downtime. Your range is important – too muted and you live a Dr Spock logical life; too extreme and you experience such intense highs and lows that you (and the people around you) won't be comfortable.

Mindfulness and gratitude

> Possibly true?
> 'You don't need more genius, you need less resistance.'
> Seth Godin

Mindfulness has become a rolling bandwagon with such momentum that it's even picking up non-believers and sceptics such as myself. This chapter is not an attempt to jump on the mindfulness bandwagon. It is born out a desire to improve our understanding of what mindfulness actually is so we can learn to steer it in the right direction.

Being mindful and 'living in the moment' are often branded as something new but, of course, they're the oldest happiness tricks in a very ancient book. Nothing is permanent. Buddhists talk of attachment and, chances are, you are attached to too many things – stuff, habits, people, thoughts, routines ...

Learning new stuff is a doddle – you are a learning machine! The difficulty arises because you are not a letting-go machine. Letting go of attachments is an interesting concept and a mightily big challenge. Buddhism has this weird juxtaposition of being incredibly simple yet somehow managing to tie you up in knots. In its purest form, Buddhism suggests you were born awesome, but you forgot. You must learn to live your life in such a way that you will remember. And then, when you remember, you can forget.

Let me untangle it. Mindfulness, at its simplest, helps you to remember that it's not enough merely being alive. You must also learn to be awake. Is that any better?

Interesting thought

'Most people treat the present moment as if it were an obstacle that they need to overcome. Since the present moment is life itself, it is an insane way to live.'

Eckhart Tolle

Mindfulness involves intentionally paying attention in the present moment, in a non-judgemental way. Bizarrely, it's the opposite of 'mind-full' – training yourself to witness the world without the usual critical commentary. It's not about running away from or supressing negative feelings or thoughts, but about relating to them from a different angle. We're back to the point of realizing that they are thoughts. They're not real. They will pass.

Living in the moment is something I've been striving to do. I *get* mindfulness, I really do. The present moment is a pretty cool place to be, the past is a gonner, the future isn't here yet, so all you have is now. I like it. But with reservations.

Humans' ability to learn from the past and imagine the future is what makes us amazing. It's why we have massive brains. So living in the moment seems almost counterintuitive or maybe even restrictive. I have some good stuff in my past so sometimes I'm quite happy there. And I feel fairly confident that my future is awesome too, so time spent imagining it makes me happy now. If I book a holiday for six months' time, I want to start enjoying it now. So I can't help feeling that living in the moment needs to be treated with a teensy bit of caution.

> ### Telling it as it is
> 'Mindfulness is simply being aware of what is happening right now without wishing it were different; enjoying the pleasant without holding onto it when it changes (which it will); being with the unpleasant without fearing it will always be this way (which it won't).'
>
> Chris Baréz-Brown

Mindfulness and gratitude are joined at the hip. The fact that you're reading this sentence means that you are richer and more educated than 99.5 per cent of people in human history. Assuming that you're in the Western world, then you currently live in the most free and tolerant society that has ever existed. Your family may frustrate you, but over a third of the world's population has only one parent and 143 million children are growing up with no parents at all.

If you've been to university, you are part of the lucky 7 per cent worldwide elite. You're unlikely to ever live at a subsistence level like almost 60 per cent of the world's population and you surely won't ever be starving like almost 25 per cent of the world population.

For decades, research has tied gratefulness and appreciation to happiness. People who are happier tend to be more grateful and appreciative for what they have. But it also works the other way around: consciously practising gratitude makes you happier. It makes you appreciate what you have and to remain in the present moment.

If you write down ten things that you appreciate but take for granted, you'll be amazed at what crops up on your list. This isn't to say you must ignore what's wrong or broken with the world. Looking out of my window, it's not white picket fences, with green fields full of grazing unicorns. As I type these words, it's grey, drizzly and I'm in a hotel in Newport. It's just to say that, when things seem shitty, don't forget what's good, true and beautiful.

Things I appreciate

1 ....

2 ....

3 ....

4 ....

5 ....

6 ....

7 ....

8 ....

9 ....

10 ....

....but accidentally take for granted!

> Fact:
> Some things are so glaringly obvious that they're hidden in plain sight.

Yesterday I ran a workshop for a newly formed group of deaf women in Derbyshire. Astonishing women, all of them. One young woman had a T-shirt emblazoned with 'Stay positive', which I thought was pretty cool. We did a selfie at the end and she confided that she didn't mind being deaf; it was her brain tumour that was causing her more grief.

Check out your list of ten and remember to shut up and be grateful.

Chapter 5
Workplace intelligence

Throughout this book I've tried to decode some academic jargon for you but this chapter still ended up feeling a little 'heavy', so, great news, I decided to top and tail it with references to The Road Runner cartoon character.

We have a peek at the four horsemen of negativity before exploring the evolution of work. I look at why you might have contracted corporate Stockholm Syndrome before getting under the skin of 'pink and fluffy', where we discover your competitive advantage. This chapter breezes through the 'multiplier effect' of leadership so you hardly notice and I ask you to compare and contrast Hitler and Gandhi.

I've translated Kim Cameron's wonderful work on 'abundance' and given my take on Simon Sinek's 'Why?' model. This chapter finishes with a précis of my Ph.D. thesis, introducing the wonderful world of the 'two-percenters', who are both highly engaged and communicative. They have gone beyond SMART, way up where they get a glorious sense of altitude sickness.

A nice but impractical idea?
'Hell, there are no rules here, we are trying to accomplish something.'
Thomas Edison

The evolution of work

Work should be nourishing. On a good day it will provide a daily filling of the lungs of Maslow's self-actualization. Breathe in all that purpose, fulfilment and self-esteem, and puff your chest out at the chance to be you at your best. Inhale the essence of inner superhero. Go make a dent in the world!

Yeah, right.

More likely, work is a chance to rent yourself out to the highest bidder for ten hours a day.

> ⏱ **Working definition:**
>
> **Fuck-off o'clock** – The end of the workday on Friday when an employee is most desperate to go home.

You can't accuse me of cutting corners to produce this chapter. I've consulted far and wide, even delving into the Wiki-God of everything to turn up some stunning facts. For example, did you know that a coyote can run twice as fast as a roadrunner? So all those times that Wile E. Coyote strapped a rocket to his back or used a giant ACME magnet in a vain attempt to catch The Road Runner, he could have just, well, *run*?

In terms of that Looney Tunes classic, I reckon that most folks are less like The Road Runner ('beep beep'), who seemed unflappably graceful in staying ahead and more like the never-quite-getting-there coyote, who overcomplicates things and lives in a state of permanent exhaustion. I hope you're not wearing that classic Wile E. face. You know the one – he's just run off the edge of a cliff and he turns to camera and shrugs, bloodshot-eyed, resigned to his fate.

I love Guy Browning's take on the modern world. Here are what he calls the 'four horsemen of negativity' – tiredness, boredom, rain and low blood sugar level. If you can tick 'yes' to any of them, you'll have 'minor glumness' in the pit of your stomach. If you can tick yes to them all (and they are very easy boxes to tick), you'll have 'irritable bastard syndrome'. The reason that is funny is because you can probably think of several 'sufferers' of this syndrome, family members or work colleagues, who are stuck in moan mode.

I'll look at families in the next chapter. For now, sit back and enjoy my take on emotional intelligence in the workplace. Let me picture your place of work – you've got a lot on, you're underpaid and are doing the work of at least three people from the olden days. Call it a lucky guess. The modern world has conspired against you so that, no matter how hard you work, there is always more to do.

There's a school of thought that says that change is nothing new. It's what we do. It's how we made it out of the swamps into the caves and how we made it out of caves into centrally-heated semi-detached houses. Darwin called it 'evolution'.

Mr Smith contracted 'irritable bastard syndrome'

What's new is the pace of it all. If you look back through history, there was a whole swathe of Middle Ages when not much happened, at least to ordinary folk. Generations of people were born, married their cousin, worked hard, prayed even harder and died young as humanity inched forwards.

Nowadays, wham, it's full-on, in-yer-face change. This book isn't meant to be an in-depth trawl through industrial history, but a bit of 'where we've come from' certainly helps us to understand 'where we are now'. In the industrial age, employees just did what they were told. The 'old' model was that the managers did the thinking and the rest of us just carried out orders. Go back a few decades and the concept of happiness at work would have seemed laughable. The unquestioned axiom was that employees weren't to be trusted and work was to be endured.

Fast forward to today and many organizations have tried to create an environment that makes work less of a chore. But beneath the skin a lack of trust remains. Employees are under surveillance like never before. Managers monitor the speed of each checkout operator. Call-centre workers have scripts to adhere to and they, the bosses, 'listen to calls for training purposes'. Do they really? Sales reps have daily and weekly targets. Schools and hospitals are inspected, with the underlying message a shrill scream of 'We don't trust you!'

> Translation:
> **Vergaderziekte** – Dutch for 'meeting sickness'.

Dan Pink talks of the need for an upgrade to a new human operating system: 'Motivation 2.0'. The old 'Motivation 1.0' software worked perfectly well back in the industrial age of command and control but nowadays it's likely that you are a knowledge worker. That means that you need to bring your brain to work. You aren't paid for your ability to shovel two tons of coal from here to over there; you're paid because of what you know, or your particular skill or your ability to find solutions to novel problems. So rather than oiling the lathe, you must take care of your own mental machinery.

Flocking to work?

In their book, *The Heart of Change: Real-life Stories of*

How People Change Their Organizations (Harvard Business Review Press, 2012), John Kotter and Dan Cohen suggest that: 'The central issue is never strategy, structure, culture, or systems. The core of the matter is always about changing the behaviour of people.'

Kotter and Cohen describe the organization as a 'complex adaptive system' – analogous to bird flocks in the natural world. The term 'emergence' sums up the idea that flocking behaviour emerges from individual behaviour. This can be difficult to get your head around at first blush, but stick with it, even if you have to read it several times. The emergent phenomenon of 'flocking' is created by the individual actions of each bird. Yet the individual action of each bird is influenced by the emergent phenomenon of the flock. They form what Kotter calls a 'complex adaptive system'.

Applied to organizations, this gives us an insight into how people create culture, but also how culture creates people in a sort of twilight zone of cultural 'neverendingness'. Yes, it's cumbersome to have to make new words up, but the alternative was 'cultural infinity', which doesn't quite portray what I'm trying to say.

> Working definition:
>
> **English** – A language that lurks in dark alleys, beats up other languages and rifles through their pockets for spare vocabulary.

Following on, that means that nobody is really 'in charge' of culture or change, no matter what it says in their job title. I've met a lot of 'change managers' and quite a few 'transformation teams' in my time. These may well be beneficial in some small way but they will not be in 'control' of change – the control lies in the hearts and minds of the people.

Pink and fluffy

I keep hearing about so-called 'soft skills', which seem to be all about the immeasurables that go with human relationships – listening, empathizing, motivating, building rapport – ingredients that make the world go round. I've also heard a lot of people dismissing these traits as a bit 'pink and fluffy', the meaning of which I hadn't considered until I just wrote that sentence. It's usually said in a disparaging tone. 'Pink and fluffy' – what does that actually mean? So I did what one does in the modern world and I Googled it and #OMG the Internet doesn't know either. You get lots of references to candyfloss and a few to unicorns and rainbows, but even the Internet is confused as to what 'pink and fluffy' actually means.

So let's explore an element of pinkness and fluffiness that I've noticed cropping up as an obsession in the modern workplace – the notion of fun. In fact, 'fun at work' has become an industry in itself, especially in the United States. Silicon Valley has firms where there are climbing walls, volleyball courts and even a yellow brick road. One US firm has a 'Wow Department' that dispatches costume-clad teams to 'surprise and delight' workers. Another US firm has a 'chief fun officer' and a 'guru of giggling'. *Yikes!*

Please don't think of me as a party pooper. I'm not *anti*-fun, but I have a suspicion that the cult of workplace happiness is driven by three popular management fads – empowerment, engagement and creativity.

There's no way I'm arguing against having these ingredients in the workplace. They are crucial if you want to stand any chance of having employees who willingly go the extra mile. My problem arises from the fact that employers often pin their hopes on 'fun' being the catalyst for these three things. It's as if 'fun' will magically make people work harder and become more creative. The problem is that 'fun' (as described above) is mixed with a large dose of coercion. Firms don't just celebrate wackiness, they require it! Behind the fun façade lies some crude management thinking – if we beat staff with the fun stick, they will work harder.

So, while I applaud happiness and believe that, where possible, work should be fun, I think organizations are coming at it for the wrong reasons. They are stimulating 'fun' because they know it creates engagement, which means people will be more productive and the results will show on the bottom line. So, to put it crudely, fun = profit.

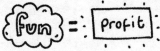

Thousands of people are living lives of screaming desperation where they work long hard hours at jobs they hate to enable them to buy things they don't need to impress people they don't like.

Nigel Marsh

Therefore, a bright and breezy company directive that it's OK to dress down on Friday might be missing the point. And a pool table in the staffroom is merely papering over the cracks of misery. The subconscious message is: 'Here's an effing pool table. It shows we care. Have some fun in your tea break and then bloody well work harder.'

You'll have heard of Stockholm Syndrome. I'll provide a definition for you and, while you're digesting it, maybe see whether you can make the link between exhausted employees working for an organization that pays the going rate and provides free gym membership.

Corporate hostages?

Stockholm Syndrome

The psychological phenomenon in which hostages express empathy and sympathy and have positive feelings towards their captors, sometimes to the point of defending and identifying with the captors.

While 'captors' and 'hostages' terminology might be a bit strong, I hope you can see my wider point. We work every hour, doing the work of three people from the old days, and yet we easily justify it in our heads.

Those organizations who really 'get it' have to shift their thinking and, yes, stand on the edge of what's possible, moving from 'creating a fun workplace because it squeezes extra productivity out of a stressed workforce' to 'creating a vibrant workplace because it's absolutely the right thing to do'. This is what's called 'metanoia', a shift of mind.

Happiness is your competitive advantage

As in all the other domains of your life, feelings are crucial at work. In business, you can explain company values until you're Smurf-faced but emotions aren't cognitive concepts. To function at its best a team needs to feel connected. We can write a set of values and stick a poster on the wall that says 'We genuinely care about our customers' and 'We treat each other with respect'. We can even put all staff through a 'values workshop' where we run them through the points on the poster. But, unless your staff *feel* like caring, the company values poster is lip service.

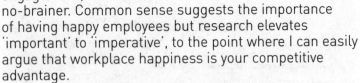

When you look at the proven benefits of employee engagement, it becomes a no-brainer. Common sense suggests the importance of having happy employees but research elevates 'important' to 'imperative', to the point where I can easily argue that workplace happiness is your competitive advantage.

Let's nip across the pond to where the 'Fortune 100 Best Companies to Work For' increased their revenues by an average of 22.2 per cent against 5 per cent for the Dow Jones Industrial Average.[23] A Hay Group Study reported that 94 per cent of the world's most admired companies believe that their efforts to engage their employees have created a competitive advantage and 85 per cent of these companies believed that their efforts to engage employees had reduced employee performance problems.[24] A University of Alberta study showed that companies that focus staff on the purpose and meaning in their positions showed a 60 per cent drop in absenteeism and a 75 per cent reduction in staff turnover.[25]

According to Shawn Achor's studies, when we are happy, our creativity triples and the likelihood of us getting promoted rises by 40 per cent, revenues grow by 37 per cent and employees' productive energy goes up by 31 per cent.[26] Positivity leads people to elevate their thinking, which gives them a wider choice of emotions and behaviours. People become less anchored in an initial hypothesis and are more willing to consider alternatives, thereby helping to move the problem from insolvable to solvable.[27]

Jessica Pryce-Jones[28] reports some extreme numbers – happy folk are 47 per cent more productive, have 180 per cent more energy, are 108 per cent more engaged, 50 per cent more motivated and have 25 per cent higher self-belief. My own statistics show that happy employees have an average of 0.6 days off per year, against the national averages of 7 and 11 days for the UK private and public sectors.

The more I dig, the more I'm beginning to think that 'soft skills' is a complete misnomer. Deriding them as pink and fluffy is about as far off the mark as you can get. What exactly is 'soft' about being able to demonstrate resilience, empathy, happiness, confidence, integrity and compassion? What is soft about being able to tune into people's emotions and get on their wavelength? What is soft about being able to use these qualities to help you adapt to the constantly changing world. Soft skills? Was somebody taking the piss? These are very hard skills indeed!

The 'multiplier effect' of leadership

Let's spend a few paragraphs digging deeper into the fluffiness. In fact, let's get under its pink exterior. If we burrow a way into emotional intelligence, what do we find?

If you're bestowed with a modicum of 'intelligence', as in the traditional sense of the word – measured by your IQ and/or exam results – then you are likely to gain entry into certain jobs. So your IQ gets you through the door. In Monopoly terms, you've passed 'Go' and can collect your cash.

However, in the context of work, academic talent is

less of a predictor of success than you might think. A Hay McBer[29] study found that the distinguishing factor between average and top performers was emotional intelligence. A top performer is 127 per cent more productive than an average performer[30] and about two-thirds of this difference is due to emotional competence. In complex jobs, this difference is more exacerbated, with Goleman reporting that in top leadership positions, more than four-fifths of the difference is due to emotional competence.[31]

The ability to build rapport with a network of key people stands out as a major factor in an article in the *Harvard Business Review*.[32] If you are socially 'out of tune', then your emails go unanswered and calls unreturned. Star performers create a network of positive connections so, when they need help, their email or phone call gets straight to the top of the list. It might not be fair and equitable but that, folks, is how the world works.

For the naysayers who argue that work is about products, services, customers and profits, I say, *Yes, of course it is!* The bigger question is: what is the route to world-class products, extraordinary service, raving fan customers and healthy profits? The short answer to that one is 'people'. Essentially, it boils down to this: *it's nigh on impossible to have world-class products and service without having people who love coming to work.*

In terms of emotional uplift, my Ph.D. shows that leadership has a 'multiplier effect'. I've encountered an awful lot of people who are dazzlingly academic but who are failing to shine. Yes, they might have more letters after their name than in their name, but emotionally they have failed to engage or inspire me.

I've sat through so many tired leadership seminars when delegates have to make a list of great leaders. The usual suspects are trotted out – Churchill, Jobs, Branson, Gates, Gandhi, King and, possibly, Hitler and Attila the Hun. There's an argument as to whether the last two were 'great leaders' and someone usually counterbalances Hitler with Jesus. And the discussion goes round in circles. They all had followers, which is pretty much the only thing they had in common. You could argue that they all had a vision. But it's a raging certainty that they all had a big dollop of luck and, crucially, they all fitted the situation at the time.

Interestingly, if you mixed and matched them, I doubt they'd have had so many followers. For example, if you'd put Gandhi in charge of 1930s Germany you'd have got a different result for sure (and a very different dress code!). Or stick Jesus as chief exec of Virgin or Attila the Hun at Apple ... or even, as history tells us, put Churchill in charge of peacetime Britain, and it all turns out a bit pants.

But looking at the characters above, it's most certainly an eclectic mix. If Hitler and Gandhi are both 'effective leaders', I'm confused.

How about if we turn our attention away from the person and towards an exact definition of 'leadership'? Well, it's easy to go around the houses on this one too! If you pick up 100 different leadership books, you'll find 100 differently nuanced definitions.

My take on it is no-nonsense: 'Leadership is about getting people to go above their job description.'

Simple as that! So whatever it is on that piece of paper that outlines, in black and white, what each person's job is, your task is to get them to do more than that. There are various ways. You could follow the slackers around with a cattle prod and every time they stop for a gossip you could give them a quick 'bzzzzt'. However tempting that sounds, the chances are it would work only while you were in close proximity: as soon as you stopped watching, their productivity would cease.

So a better and more humane way of getting staff to go the extra mile is to get them to want to, and that brings me squarely back to the battery of 'soft skills'. And these soft skills give a massive clue to where 'leadership' actually comes from. Daniel Goleman is the founding father of emotional intelligence and I think he articulates it rather nicely in this quote:

'Great leaders move us. They ignite our passion and inspire the best in us. When we try to explain why they are so effective, we speak of strategy, vision, or powerful ideas. But the reality is much more primal: Great leadership works through the emotions.'

Putting the 'why' into organizations

Focusing on the best – those that Kim Cameron terms 'positively deviant' – is an interesting project. Who are the ones that really shine? I set myself the task of unearthing the gems – the sparkly people who have more upbeat-ness than most but not so much that you want to test their positivity with a rabbit punch to the side of the head – 'Find an upside in that, you happy-clappy charlatan.'

I call the genuine uplifting minority, the 'two-percenters', a term that doesn't appear in the Ph.D. but is something I use as shorthand for the folk who carry a feel-good factor with them.

So, playing the yes/no game, here are a few things that will quieten the doubting in your head:

- *Yes*, it's difficult to get it exactly right and nobody nails it every time. It's OK to be imperfect.

- *No*, it's not about fixing an inane grin on your face and pretending you're happy when you're not. It's OK to have some downtime.

- *Yes*, there's effort involved in being standout uplifting (because you are lifting yourself *and* those around you).

- And, *yes*, the effort is totally worthwhile...

- ...Because, *yes*, it's probably the most important skill you will ever learn.

All those bite-sized points are important but none more so than the last one. Being the kind of person who inspires those around them is absolutely a *learned* behaviour. Sure, there is a bit of genetic jiggery-pokery that improves your odds, and your circumstances can help (e.g., it's easier to be upbeat if you're in a job that plays to your strengths) but a massive chunk of your happiness and effervescence is directly under your control.

An interesting notion

'You're only given one little spark of madness. You mustn't lose it.'

Robin Williams

I compared two-percenters with the people they were sitting next to and it got me wondering. They're working in the same team, for the same pay, with the same pressures and the same manager, so the difference can't be external – it must be internal.

Brace yourself for a sentence that is bigger than it sounds. Being a two-percenter is a *portable benefit*. By that, I mean it is much less about your job and much more about who you are. Back to plain simple no-nonsense language: a positive person will be a positive person almost irrespective of what job they're doing. The person brings their effervescence with them.

This is a real downer for organizational strategists and designers who have spent zillions on creating a fabulous working environment because what I'm saying is that employee engagement isn't about gym membership or a pool table in the staffroom. Inspiration isn't ever really 'top–down' or 'bottom–up', but 'inside–out'.

In terms of knowing where to start with inside–out change, I believe it is with a single word, 'Why?' There are numerous ways in which you can engage your colleagues but most will fail unless you first grapple with why you and your colleagues come to work at all.

This links with Simon Sinek's amazingly simple concept of the 'Golden Circle'.[33] His model is represented below.

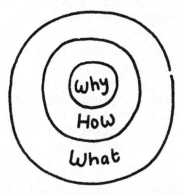

Source: Simon Sinek, *Start with Why: How Great Leaders Inspire Everyone to Take Action* (Penguin, 2009).

Too many people start at the outside of the circle and work inwards. So, for example, I'd expect every member of your team to know *what* their job is and *how* they go about it. But a strong and compelling *why* is often the missing link. Indeed, if you can find a good 'why', the 'how' and 'what' will look after themselves.

Abundance

I rather like what Kim Cameron calls a 'culture of abundance' – a nirvana state that is well worth going for. It starts with a vibrancy and aliveness that make staff feel valued. Cameron & Winn talk about 'virtuous organizations', which are characterized by collective displays of moral excellence by employees. They articulate it thus: 'Employees collectively behave in ways that are consistent with the best of the human condition and the highest aspirations of humankind.'[34]

Then Cameron discovered and ran with Gretchen Spreitzer and Scott Sonenshein's notion of 'positive deviance': 'intentional behaviours that depart from the norms of a referent group in honourable ways'.[35] Keeping it simple, positively deviant behaviours stand out for all the right reasons and in business parlance staff willingly 'go the extra mile'.

However, in the hothouse of business where managers are judged on results, they end up focusing on preventing bad things from happening. This distinction is subtle but highly significant. All businesses want excellence, but it is how they go about achieving it that is interesting. So-called 'deficit organizations' are focused on achieving consistency by solving or preventing errors. They create rules/procedures/policies to achieve minimum standards. This is aimed at stopping mistakes but it has the unintended by-product of clipping the wings of the awesome staff.

Cameron explains that organizational virtuousness refers to behaviours that extend beyond what is normally expected. In the continuum below, normality or healthy performance is at the mid-point with positively and negatively deviant performance located at the polar extremes of the continuum. Essentially, you can stand out at either end of the spectrum; negative deviance represents eye-wateringly abhorrent deviation from the norm and positive deviance is standout amazing.

Here is Cameron's model, but with my categories and language superimposed on it:

	Negative deviance	Normal	Positive deviance
Staff wellness	Illness	Health	Vitality
Staff morale	Demoralized	Living for the weekends	Buzzing
Business effectiveness	Struggling	Good	World class
Efficiency	Busy fools	Busy	A busy hive
Quality of output	Insipid	In line with expectations	Wow!
Change readiness	Stuck	Coping	Responsive
Staff engagement	'Presenteeism' (staff are there in body)	A mix of good and bad days	Enthusiasm burns brightly
Customer engagement	An unsupportive lot	A handful of the usual faces	Thriving
'Atmosphere'	Victim	Surviving	Flourishing
Leadership style	Controlling. Driven by fear	Empowering (in words only)	Inspiring. Driven by possibilities

Source: Based on Kim Cameron's 'Deviance Continuum.'[36]

Most managers are driven by the fear of slipping into the red zone, so pay almost exclusive attention to the gap between what is going wrong (mistakes, poorly performing departments, customer complaints, etc.) and the middle point on the continuum. This gap might be labelled a 'deficit gap' or a 'problem solving gap'. A large majority of scientific research in fields such as medicine, psychology and organizational studies focuses on deficit gaps such as overcoming problems and grappling with angry customers and underperforming staff.

Often, the gap between the middle of the continuum (healthy functioning) and the right side (positive deviance) goes unexplored. This 'abundance gap' represents the difference between successful and extraordinarily positive performance and is, quite frankly, worthy of some attention. Closing the abundance gap requires that leaders focus not only on being effective, efficient or reliable in performance but on being 'extraordinary'. Close this particular gap and your stakeholders (staff, customers, suppliers) will be saying 'Wow!'

Cameron calls this the 'abundance approach' and you don't stand a cat-in-hell's chance of achieving it by doing what everyone else is doing.

Smells like team spirit

Selection policy for multiple World Cup-winning New Zealand All Blacks

'No dickheads!'

The modern workforce is so often full-throttle, characterized by an industrious frenzy that acts as a wormhole to a panic-ridden universe where you are excused from contemplating or pondering. Busyness offers up an emotional escape hatch. When everything is a crisis, what's a person to do except throw themselves into it? After all, isn't that the right thing to do?

You've probably worked in an organization where you felt you were going through the motions. I'm also hoping that you've experienced the opposite – of working in a team where work didn't feel like work. The place was buzzing, you felt totally energized and, whisper it quietly, you would probably have worked there for free. Yes, that last bit is a bit strong – you've got a mortgage to pay and mouths to feed – but I'm hoping you get my drift. Some teams are a joy and a pleasure to be part of.

There's a small probability that high-performance teams might happen spontaneously. But you can improve the odds by lighting the blue touchpaper and standing back. In fact, the 'standing back' is rather crucial. I have never met anyone who comes to work to deliberately do a bad job or have a stinking attitude. We all want to shine and give our best but it's often the rules, systems or manager that gets in the way. My advice to leaders is always to *get out of the way.* Stop trying to motivate people – it doesn't work. In fact, a little counterintuitively, it's not your job to motivate people. Your job is to *be motivated*.

There are various definitions of 'engagement', my favourite being this very simple one: 'feeling responsible for, and committed to, superior job performance so that job performance matters to the individual'.[37] It implies a sense of focus, emotional investment, effort and a concern for outcomes. Further, when actively engaged in our work we are more likely to feel good, competent and have a sense of belonging.[38] Rather like motivation, engagement cannot be commanded. Losada & Heapy suggest it starts with connectivity and that the ratio of positive to negative is the single most important factor in predicting team performance. In case you're interested, high-performing teams have a ratio of six positives to every negative, with medium performance at two to one and low-performing teams the other way around at three negatives to every positive.[39]

If we accept these implications, it suggests that offering positive comments is more than a nice-to-have, it's an imperative necessity for high performance. Summing up the various findings, it appears that a positivity to negativity ratio of between 3:1 and 11:1 is good, whereas above 30:1 is dysfunctional, creating an unproductive cosy mutual love-in, once again proving that everything (even positivity) is damaging in excess.

Revisiting the soft skills from earlier, it's my belief that most of the really important things in a business can't really be measured. Try measuring creativity, excitement, commitment, buzz, happiness, confidence, team spirit or love. I'd argue that in a team, as in a family, it's the things that can't be counted that actually count the most. Intuitively, we know this but the system dictates otherwise and Peter Drucker's maxim of 'what gets measured gets done' rings true. In simple terms, managers spend so much of their time on the metrics that they sometimes take their eye off the factors that contribute to world-class metrics – the people!

This brings me to the vexed issue of goal setting. This is a personal bugbear of mine so apologies in advance if this sounds like me addressing you from my high horse. I'm of the opinion that a goal should scare you a little and excite you a lot. Here in the UK we are smitten with SMART objectives. My updated take on this arthritic-kneed acronym is:

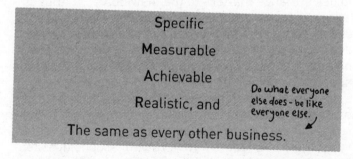

Specific

Measurable

Achievable

Realistic, and   *Do what everyone else does - be like everyone else.*

The same as every other business.

So SMART goals are absolutely fine so long as you want to be like every other business. Do you really want to just go through the motions? I hand-on-heartedly cannot think of any major breakthrough in human thinking that would have ever been achieved with a SMART objective. Imagine if, in the 1950s, there had been a meeting at NASA, populated by people who'd bought into 'SMART'. At the 'any other business' part some bright young thing would have raised their hand, cleared their throat and suggested: 'Why don't we send someone to the Moon?' The SMART brigade would have guffawed. 'Gee, buddy, have you any idea how far that is?'

But if you want to be world class, and I'm deadly serious about this, you have to raise your gaze above what everyone else is doing. Putting someone on the Moon is what I call a HUGG – a Huge Unbelievably Great Goal – or what Kim Cameron calls an 'Everest Goal'.[40]

Top tip

Everest

What a wonderful analogy. An Everest goal is massive and inspirational. Has Everest been conquered before? Yes, but not by very many. It's just about doable, but the enormity of the goal means that it's achieved only through world-class performance and teamwork. HUGGs are exciting, stimulating and ever so slightly uncomfortable. They're on the edge of achievability and, most importantly, they're worth getting out of bed for.

Interesting thought

'Being realistic is the most commonly travelled road to mediocrity. Why would you be realistic? What's the point of being realistic? It's unrealistic to walk into a room and flick a switch and lights come on. That's unrealistic. Fortunately, Edison didn't think so.'

Will Smith

My research shows that 'setting huge goals' and 'playing to your strengths' are two sides of the same coin. Let me explain. It's nigh on impossible to achieve huge goals unless you and your team are playing to their strengths. And, it's a waste of time bothering to play to your strengths if you are aiming for a piddling SMART objective. You'll overshoot it by a mile.

Focusing on weaknesses will lead to competence whereas focusing on strengths will lead to extraordinary performance. Alex Linley purports that when people use their strengths they become engaged, energized and authentic, suggesting that realizing strengths can be the smallest thing that is likely to make the biggest difference to workplace performance because of its impact on so many aspects of sustainable improvement. He talks of dialling your strengths up or down to achieve what he calls 'the golden mean' – that is, the right strength in the right amount in the right way at the right time.[41]

And while our heads are telling us this makes perfect sense, the reality is that all too often we get somewhat hung up on our weaknesses. If you think about it, it's an odd state of affairs in which we recruit team members because they are right for the job and then spend the next 20 years working out what they're not very good at and sending them on courses to eradicate their weaknesses.

Tom Rath reports that an employee whose supervisor focuses on her strengths is more than 2.5 times as likely to be engaged as one whose supervisor focuses on her weaknesses.[42] Harter, Schmidt & Hayes found that work units that offered opportunities to focus on strengths were significantly more engaged.[43] The Corporate Leadership Council showed that focusing on strengths increased performance by 36.4 per cent while focusing on weaknesses made performance decline by 26.8 per cent.[44]

Getting the exact mix of connectivity, huge goals and strengths is more of an art than a science. Pulling the strands together, this is less about how many qualifications you have and more about creating a set of positive feelings in which people have the skills matched with a genuine passion for wanting to be world class.

So how do you know when you've hit that sweet spot? Well, this is when you venture into the state of 'flow', or what athletes might call 'the zone' – where you achieve effortless high performance.

> Quote about flow from someone who knows
>
> 'You feel different. It's positive thought after positive thought. You aren't even thinking about it you just go out and do it. I'm lucky enough to have had that feeling a lot of times throughout my career.'
>
> Rory McIlroy

You know when you're in the flow zone because time flies as you apply your best self to the problem and, rather than exhausting you, the job makes you feel alive.

Coming full circle, The Road Runner and Wile E. Coyote were both living life fast, but only one was living it well.

Chapter 6

Family intelligence

In a humdinger of a chapter, we take the science of positive emotions into the home, via dysentery in Java and cornflakes in Sydney. I paint an idyllic picture of wholesome family life (think *The Waltons*) before examining what it's really like, from lots of perspectives. We stereotype Mum as the superhero – kin-keeper, emotional-broker and sufferer of the dreaded '6 o'clock crash'.

Then there's Dad who, in school report terms, 'could do better!' And how about the teenagers? They have a role-less role and suffer from peer pressure like never before.

So, the big question is this: if family life is a soup, what flavour are you adding?

The chapter finishes with my top ten parenting tips, which are more scientific than they might at first appear. They veer from the sublime 'gazing lovingly' to the almost ridiculous 'putting your teenager in charge of the utility bills'. Oh, and the 'seven-second hug' might just change your life.

'As a child, Zaphod had been diagnosed with ADHDDAAADHD (ntm) ABT which stood for Always Dreaming His Dopey Days Away, Also Attention Deficit Hyperflactulance Disorder (not to mention) A Bit Thick.'

Eoin Colfer, describing the Douglas Adams character
Zaphod Beeblebrox in *And Another Thing ...* (Penguin, 2009)

The general rule of parenting is that your children won't do what you say, but they will do what you do.

You, the blue dot

That's you + me!

Many years ago I did the 'take a year off and go backpacking around the world' thing. The good news is that, yes, I found myself. And the not-so-good news is that I found dysentery, too. Having lost four months and three stones in South-East Asia, I was rather excited to be on a flight to Oz. It was early morning as we touched down in Sydney. I grabbed a bus to town, checked into a youth hostel and tucked into a bowl of cornflakes and fresh pasteurized milk. That was my first non-rice meal for a very long time and was greedily guzzled. Eventually, I removed my chin from the bowl and looked around. I did a double-take at the huge world map that adorned the wall – Australia was in the middle. *How bizarre!* Shunting Oz to centre stage had moved the UK to top left, where America should be. And America had popped up on the right. I pondered that map for quite a while without realizing I would end up writing about it 30 years later.

In the intervening period, the Internet was born and Google Maps has become a staple smartphone app. In the unlikely event that you don't have it, you open the app, lock on to some satellites and the app tells you where you are. You appear as a blue dot. You then tap in where you'd like to go and Google plots a route. You walk or drive, following the progress of you, the blue dot.

Rather like the Australians putting themselves at the centre of their world, the blue dot is how you live your life. You are, quite naturally, focused on yourself. Sure, you look out for others but the world is processed and interpreted by you. In fact, you are basically a massive information processor. You are the centre of your universe. And because of the way your mind works, you sort of assume that you are the centre of everybody else's universe, too. But, of course, you're not. Everybody is their own blue dot – the epicentre of their own world.

This has colossal implications for relationships across the board. Each person is their own blue dot. They have an identity, a self-image, some strengths and a whole load of insecurities running through their mind. The more you can find out about this blue dot the better your chance of a positive relationship.

Brains are much more active developmentally in childhood. The first two years are characterized by crazy growth. Learning to talk, walk and control your bowels – these are massive social skills that a couple of my mates struggle with but, fingers crossed, you will have mastered early on. Two million new connections are formed every second in an infant's brain. By age two, a child has over one hundred trillion synapses – double the number an adult has. In fact, up to seven years old the brain is a massive ever-expanding Jell-O of connectivity at which point it has peaked and has far too many connections. It will never be able to use them all so, as it reaches full bloom, the brain stops creating more connections and sets about pruning the ones it has. As you mature, 50 per cent of your synapses will be pruned back.[45]

There's another massive spurt of development during adolescence and then your brain progressively solidifies. Your mature brain is in place by your mid-20s so, after that, you're probably better off devoting time to working out how to get the best out of it rather than trying to regrow it.

Let me be clear. Your early years are crucial. Brain growth occurs in such a way as it develops a stupid amount of axons, dendrites and connections. Up until the age of about seven, you are a universe of possibilities. And, gradually, depending on your early years' experiences, these possibilities get narrowed down. For me, there are two standout points here:

1. Although the rate of development slows, your brain never stops changing. It is a relentless shape-shifter, constantly rewiring its own circuitry.

2. The process of becoming who you are is less to do with what pathways grow in your brain and much more about what pathways get lopped off.

A family affair

If you're of a certain age, you might remember the TV series *Little House on the Prairie* and its equally wholesome cousin, *The Waltons*, with their classic clean-cut wholesome family units. Every episode was basically the same. The central tenet was that the family was happy, something rocked their boat, the family held together and through mutual love they pulled through in the end. They were poor but, my goodness, they were happy and dependable units of close-knit kinship.

You tend not to get this type of programme now; in fact, the opposite rules apply. TV luxuriates in shows about dysfunctional families who shout a lot. I can't remember the last time I saw a TV series in which a family sat around a huge table, reflecting on the moral lessons of the day while tucking into generous helpings of hearty home-made pumpkin pie before a cheery 'Night, Jim Bob'.

However, despite the dysfunction (or maybe in spite of it) there are several rules of great parenting that we can glean from the science of emotional wellbeing.

Relationships between parents and their offspring are now judged on closeness and warmth whereas in the not-too-distant past the quality of feelings was secondary to the child's good behaviour. Parents were encouraged to adopt a stern and authoritarian posture. In the early twentieth century the official advice was not to play with your children lest you become too familiar, and it wasn't until the mid-1950s that psychologists began advocating warmth, closeness and shared fun.[46] I think I'm on fairly safe territory in suggesting that family warmth and cohesion are deemed more than a nice-to-have, but actually regarded as essential.

An important starting point, and one that is often missed, is to have a look at the world from the perspectives of different family members. Remember, each is their own blue dot, focusing on their little world.

Let's start with women. Rewind to the nineteenth century and there was a strong probability that the matriarch worked in the fields and nurtured children – the equivalent of today's super-mum. As is still the case in many countries today, women gave birth in the morning and were back in the fields by the afternoon. Life was brutal. Rural–urban migration in the late nineteenth century changed all that. The woman's role, in theory at least, became one of creating a happy home. It was all a bit 'tea-on-the-table-when-he-gets-home' kind of thing. During the Second World War women proved what was already known – they were superheroes. The men went off to fight and women took on the factory jobs. In movie terms, it was a transition from *The Stepford Wives to Flashdance* – from the 'perfectly domesticated wife' to 'working in an armaments factory', thus redefining the nature of women. It must have been a bit galling when, after the war, women, despite having proved their worth, were asked to step aside to provide jobs for the boys.

Nowadays, family life is under discussion once more.

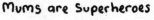

Mums are Superheroes

Women experience something called 'the 6 o'clock crash', an overwhelming feeling of frustration over the fact that, after a hard day's work, more hard work lies ahead.[47]

The mum is also the 'kin-keeper', the person who maintains contacts with wider family and neighbours. If there are children, it'll be the mum who knows the other mums. She'll likely know the names of the children's school friends, too. Mothers are likely to be strongly invested in their family role – they have been socialized to see it as who they are – so are invested in a role that is inherently draining. The paradox is that the mother's role is to create a happy home but that the exhaustion of being the family linchpin means that she might not be happy playing that role.[48]

There's always going to be an element of 'Well, it's not like that in my house' and I acknowledge that I'm painting a broad-brush picture. Yes, there might be a legion of super-dads out there but the truth is that men are hardly waiting, Dysons at the ready, to take on an equal share of the household burden. Husbands do not increase their share of the housework even if wives work full time. Plus, one academic reports on something that I can attest to be the case in our house: that in some cases men perform housework so badly that women have to do it over again.[49]

I've stereotyped mums so let's do the same to dads. Traditional men, according to the stereotype, are calm, rational and rarely swayed by emotion. In times gone by, this stolid patriarchal, 'Wait till your father gets home' approach meant that the dad acted as disciplinarian. Indeed, it is this apparent ability to be 'uncluttered by emotions' that meant men were deemed to be in charge of countries and families.[50] So, emotional detachment was the way things were. It's what men saw other men doing and the meme was passed down through the generations. Please note, I'm not trawling though history from the year dot – this is fairly recent stuff.

Indeed, parenting books of the 19th & 20th centuries virtually ignored fathers[51]. The Puritans believed fathers were called by God to enforce absolute obedience, with the goal of breaking the child's will.[52] While some may be nostalgic for discipline and respect, I think your specs would need a very heavy coat of rose-tinting to go back to these particular 'good old days'.

It's a sad statistic but apparently modern fathers have roughly three minutes a day of conversation with their children. If that's not shameful enough, evidence suggests the valuable three minutes is restricted in scope and colour so, whereas mums tend to chat about friends, family and school, dads tend to chat about sport or ask 'How was your day?'[53]

Dad then sits in the dominant armchair, guarding the remote, flicking through the channels, which annoys the females greatly. It transpires that 35 per cent of daughters say dads meet their emotional needs, as compared to 72 per cent for mums.[54] So, if this were a school report, dads would find 'Must do better!' on pretty much every page. Superhero-style pants on the outside might be a step too far (though, bearing in mind you are already an embarrassment to your teenager, it probably wouldn't matter a great deal) but dads need to learn to maximize their role. In healthy family functioning, it's the fathers who deviate most from the norm. Let me say this as simply as I can: pretty much across the board, mums are superheroes. In the happiest families, it is the dad that also steps up to the plate. Here we go back to pink fluffiness but the best dads are aware of their own feelings and less likely to walk through the door and dump their emotional garbage on those closest to them. They are also less likely to withdraw from difficult social situations so, yes, the dog needs walking, but it will have to wait.[55]

This applies to both mums and dads but I'm aiming it more at dads because they are the ones who need to pull their parenting socks up – *the bit when you come home from work is crucial.* The concept of 'para-sympathetic arousal' means that your family will catch your emotions. In a bizarre tradition, many families go through a ritual of offloading all their emotional detritus on the ones they love most in life. Saving up all your rubbish to brag about seems like a strange thing to do but, nevertheless, it's very often what happens. If this habit occurs day after day, it has a cumulative effect on family wellbeing.

Negative emotions work a bit like second-hand smoke – you catch them whether you want to or not. Also, it's not just the inevitability of the transfer, there's also a flavour. Daniel Goleman calls it 'emotional soup', the concept that, in any social situation, everyone is adding a certain 'flavour' of feelings.

Two things spring to mind: first, dare to ask yourself what flavour you are adding. Are you coming through the door with joy and enthusiasm or are you poisoning the family atmosphere with toxicity? And, second, not all family members are equal. Yes, everyone is adding something to the emotional soup but, as a parent, you are adding the most. For 'parent' read 'leader without a title' – your emotional contagion is massive. Please note, I am not pontificating about you *finding* your impact or *experimenting* with it; I am screaming that *you are already having it*. This is a less-than-gentle reminder for you to wield your impact in a positive way.

Dads need to pull up their parenting ones!

Applying the same history lesson to teenagers, it seems that their emotional experience has also been shaped by cultural forces. Before mass industrialization, the time and energies of young people were tied up with family duties – they either worked on the smallholding, helped in the house or were farmed out as apprentices at a young age, with (unquestionably) all income channelled back to the family.

The Industrial Revolution required dads to go out to work and it also necessitated children to receive a secondary education. They were no longer tied to the family unit. Their teenage years were now spent in school with peers of the same age; hence their 'peer group' began to have a massive influence. It doesn't take much imagination to see that teenagers' allegiance became skewed away from the family and more towards their peers.

There is a paradox at the heart of modern-day youth – as teenagers have become free from family duties, they are now burdened with major life changes at an earlier age. They have less defined responsibilities in what one academic calls a 'roleless role'.[56] Arguably, they may have lost a lack of purpose. And, through all this, they are going through a spurt of development that young people have gone through for ever, an injection of hormones that changes what and how they experience the world. Adolescents develop abstract and critical reasoning skills and, although these skills represent psychological growth, they actually heighten children's sensitivity to life. These advanced reasoning skills allow them, for the first time, to see beneath the surface of situations and envision hidden threats to their wellbeing. They begin to imagine what peers think about them and become more self-consciousness in the process, sometimes imploding inwards towards the blue dot.

So, if men are from Mars and women from Venus, what planet are your modern teenagers from? 'Glum' perhaps, or 'Planet Whatevs'? Willard Andrew Collins suggests that these different family perspectives are greater during adolescence than at any other period, a time when innocent parental comments can be misinterpreted as vicious personal attacks.[57] In a rather unfair way, mothers are especially affected by these changing moods, especially those of their daughters with the data suggesting that transmission is one-way – mothers pick up what children feel but teens are less likely to pick up their mum's moods.[58] Mum is the 'emotional broker', the person who is most attentive to the family tone.[59]

Personally, I find all this complex spaghetti-relationships stuff intensely interesting. But, thusfar, I've suggested that we're all blue dots from different planets but have fallen short of offering any cast-iron advice.

So, strap yourself in and away we go on a whistle-stop

tour of the top ten brilliant parenting rules gleaned from the science of positive emotions ...

Rule #1: 8:1

The modern take is that you should be helping your child nurture a growth mindset. Coercive behaviour (punishment and pointing out what's wrong) activates a behavioural inhibition system where kids stick to what they know to be safe. Over time, coercive parenting leads to a fixed mindset and your child becomes focused on not making mistakes. If you mix in a healthy dose of positive reinforcement, you will be rewarded with discretionary effort. It encourages 'approach behaviours' such as creativity, innovation and exploration and, best of all, it builds a growth mindset – an optimistic frame of mind in which your child starts to explore the outer reaches of their comfort zone.

> **Top tip**
> 'Celebrate what you want to see more of.'
> Tom Peters

One of the most effective things a parent and/or grandparent can do is to use a positivity/negativity ratio of about 8:1. It can be difficult to get it right, but catch your child doing things well. Notice the little things and tell them. Oh, and mean it!

Rule #2: Gaze lovingly

If you've got young children, here's a belter from Gretchen Rubin. You know how last thing at night can be a mad rush, dashing around getting school bags sorted, packed lunches packed and school uniforms ironed? Instead of rushing around headless-chicken style, why not indulge in a spot of what Gretchen calls 'gazing lovingly'. Gretchen and her husband say: 'Come on, let's go and gaze lovingly at the kids as they sleep.'

That is such a fabulous idea: simple, free and a perfect example of being in the moment.

Rule #3: Celebrate better

Shelly Gable suggests that how we celebrate is a strong predictor of relationship strength.[60] Seligman (who is pretty much the godfather of positive psychology) agrees that how we behave in a moment of triumph and joy makes a huge difference in either building or undermining relationships and that there are four types of response when you hear some good news.

For example, at the dinner table, your child announces that they've got down to the final three in the auditions for the lead role in the school play. Here are the four responses in table form:

	Passive	Active
Constructive	'That's great news, and about time. They should have given you a chance ages ago.'	'That's amazing. How do you feel? How did they tell you? How did you react? Tell me more ...'
Destructive	'Oh, can you pass the salt?'	'Yikes. The pressure! What if you don't get it?'

I'm hoping you are already avoiding the passive/destructive!

Once again, the aim here is to raise your levels of enthusiasm while retaining your authenticity. I'm not suggesting an over-the-top punching-of-the-air celebration for every smidgen of good news, but a raising of your levels of enthusiasm means that you won't miss out on so many glorious relationship-building opportunities. My old responses were along the lines of 'Nice one! I'm proud of you', which sat firmly in the realms of 'passive constructive'. I meant it and it was heartfelt, but on reflection it was born out of busyness and being preoccupied with my own blue dot. So I've experimented with upping my levels of enthusiasm from 'lukewarm' to 'seriously hot'. The 'active constructive' reaction is completely brilliant on all sorts of levels. Rather than spelling it out, I'll let you experiment by celebrating success and good news in your own consciously uplifted way. Ultimately, it's not about your thoughts and feelings, it's about helping others revel in theirs.

They're proud and you're proud. Your active constructive response means that they know you're proud. Best of all, you've engineered it so you know they know you're proud. The result is that everyone feels great and they will want to repeat that behaviour.

Read it again, maybe a couple of times, until it sinks in!

An uplifting joke

'So I was getting into my car, and this bloke says to me "Can you give me a lift?". I said: "Sure, you look great, the world's your oyster, go for it."'

Tim Vine

Rule #4: Praise for effort rather than talent

Carol Dweck's book is crammed with good advice.[61] One of her experiments involved setting a group of children a really stern exam after which one group was praised for intelligence ('You are sooo clever!') and the other for effort ('You've worked reaaally hard!').

Next, she set a test that was impossible for them to complete. The first group (praised for being clever) soon capitulated, figuring that they weren't clever enough, but the second group (praised for effort) stuck at it and outperformed the others by 30 per cent. Dweck's advice is that, if your child accomplishes something, don't say, 'Well done, you are such a little genius!' but rather, 'Awesome, you put the effort in and got the reward.'

Here's a concrete example. If your daughter scores a goal at football, don't high-five her and say, 'Holy cow, total genius girl. You were born to play football.' You'd be better off saying, 'Amazing goal. That's what practice and hard work gets you!' and ruffle her hair in a chummy fashion.

Or when your son wins an award for art: 'Crikey, young man, you are destined to be the next Picasso.' Nope. 'That's what you get for all those hours of hard work.' Yep.

Rule #5: Never pay your children for chores or exam results

NEVER reward exam results like this

Here's another pearler, this time from Dan Pink. He says that you shouldn't pay your kids to do chores and on no account should you bribe them with cash for exam results. According to Dan, it's a slippery slope that kills their work ethic and love of learning. Let's examine the subtext of your well-meaning 'payment by results' system, carefully devised in consultation with your child. What you are effectively saying is: 'I understand that studying is a horrible thing to do. And I appreciate that you will only do it for money.' And bang goes their love of learning. You are teaching them (albeit innocently and subconsciously) that learning is a chore. Similarly with the payment-for-chores arrangement. On one level, it makes perfect sense. The teenager's part of the bargain is to keep their room tidy, empty the dishwasher and empty the bins. Payment is effectively bribing them to comply with what is an essential family maxim: that we all muck in just like the Waltons did.

Rule #6: Utility savings are theirs

Doctor: Your dad's been in a coma for nine days. We're running out of ideas.

Me: Let me try. [goes to adjust thermostat and turns it up by four degrees]

Dad: [opens one eye]

Give pocket money in one lump sum. Yes, controversial I know, but they have to learn how to allocate it, which is an essential lifeskill. Or, when they're a little older, present them with an electricity or gas bill

£1000 P.money

One lump sum

that shows them how much it costs to heat and light the house. If, for argument's sake, the bill is £1,000, tell them that, if next year's bill is less than that, they can keep the difference. In a bizarre reversal of the normal routine, it will be *them* following *you* around the house switching lights off!

'Turn the lights off Dad!'

I'm tempted to stop at Rule #6 because this is the best one ever, but, no, there are some other nuggets coming.

Rule #7: 'I wish you well'

Dr Amit Sood[62] created something that sounds rather like a football team formation, what he terms the '5-3-2 technique'.

You must first consider five people that you're grateful to have in your life. Then, for the first three minutes you meet them like a long-lost friend without judgement or trying to improve them. And, says the doc, for the first two seconds when you see anyone, send them a silent 'I wish you well'. It's rather beautiful.

Rule #8: The seven-second hug

Hug it out!

This goes hand in hand with the above. I started delving into the research behind this and then thought, sod it, nobody cares what the statistics say. Here's the headline news – the average hug lasts just over two seconds. If you hang on for a full seven seconds, then oodles of nice warm chemicals flow around both bodies and the love is transferred. Worth buying this book just for this top tip!

A piece of advice: don't count out loud while you're doing the seven-second hug as it tends to spoil the effect.

Rule #9: Chatter away!

I once overheard a very scary conversation at the school gates. A grandma was cooing at a baby in a pram, indulging in one of those 'Ooh, you are such a sweet and bonnie girl in your matching pink hat and gloves' moments, and the mother replied, 'Why are you speaking to the baby? She can't even speak back.'

Experienced head teachers have told me that kids are arriving in reception class unable to speak. Not 'unable' as in 'quiet and shy' but as in 'they don't know how' because they've never been spoken to! You're astounded and slightly shocked by this revelation but, once the thought settles, you're probably not altogether surprised.

Academic papers and government reports show us that far too many families are hindering their children's development. Language, as Alva Noe suggests, '... is a shared cultural practice that can only be learned by a person who is one among many in a special kind of cultural eco-system'.[63] Behind this ever so slightly too complicated sentence is the proposition that working-class homes tend to be quieter – *much quieter*. A study by Hart & Risley[64] suggested that, by age four, children raised in poorer families will have heard 32 million *fewer* words than children raised in professional families. To add to the woe, it's not just quantity, it's also the emotional tone.

So please speak a lot and, where possible, couch your language in the 8:1 ratio of positive to negative. Instead of saying 'How was school?' why not upgrade to 'What was the highlight of your day?' or 'What was the funniest or most amazing thing you've done today?' Say it like you mean it and, of course, listen properly to the answer. You will be rewarded with an increased likelihood of a positive conversation.

Rule #10: Celebrate strengths

Parents have a lot to answer for. Too much love and encouragement gives you an inflated idea of what you can do. Witness the early rounds of the prime-time talent shows where the kid has been bigged up so much that they believe the parental hype. We, the viewer, reach for our earplugs as the performer refuses to accept the truth of their wailing banshee voice. And yet too little love and encouragement means that we're crippled emotionally. You can have the best voice on the planet but no confidence to get up there and belt it out.

A lot of people beat themselves up about what they're not good at to the point that it stops them celebrating what they are good at. Be a strengths spotter.

So, there you go, my top ten family-friendly tips to create a harmonious and loving family atmosphere. There are no guarantees but you will be loading the dice in your favour. If I were going to sneak in an extra tip, then Rule #11 might be to learn to make pumpkin pie to create the ultimate Waltons-themed evening.

In summing up this chapter, I will, once again, defer to Kim Cameron. He may use some big words and phrases, like 'affirmative bias' and 'heliotropic effect', but, at their heart, his principles are total genius. Put simply, an affirmative bias is an orientation towards your child's strengths rather than their weaknesses, optimism rather than pessimism and support rather than criticism.

And the heliotropic effect? Well, that's the biological tendency in which 'all living things grow towards that which gives life and away from that which depletes life'. In short, all living things have an inclination towards positivity. Plants lean towards the light. Kids lean towards encouragement. I'm struggling to find anything that I can say that is simpler or more enlightening than this.

mmm... pumpkin pie

Chapter 7

Thought intelligence

The biggie! Switch off your judgometer and settle down for the chapter of a lifetime.

First up, the easy stuff – willpower. It's a muscle and it gets tired.

Next up, the heavy stuff – you are not and never will be a cucumber. I would imagine that's quite a relief. This chapter dares to delve into beliefs and consciousness, before reversing the normal question of 'What do I need to do to make me happy?' to 'What suffering am I willing to endure to make me happy?'.

And then we disappear into the Wonderland of thought, via the musings of a wise Glaswegian welder. Reality? What on earth is it? And where's its source? The truth is that you can feel nothing without thought and the best place to start is right now. If you don't believe me, just ask my boyz.

Yes, dear reader, you're best off suspending disbelief and, if you're proper clever, check your academic baggage into the hold. You might have to read this chapter a couple of times but, here we go – 'thought intelligence' in all its glory. Chocks away …

There may be some aspects of life that we cannot control absolutely; however, thoughts do not fall into this category.

Dr. Steve G. Jones

Willpower versus 'won't-power'

A request. Please switch off your intellect and just absorb the ideas in this chapter. It's a paradoxical mix of the astoundingly simple and excruciatingly complex, a collision of the planets of academia, philosophy and common sense, culminating in a

massive Big Bang of obviousness. So don't try too hard. I'll do all the work. Just relax and be ready for anything.

If it gets tough, which it will, my advice is hang on in there. Remember, this chapter has been crafted for you, whatever your current level of knowledge. It's been 49 years in the making and is, by some margin, the best chapter I've written yet. Despite that, some readers will not like it one little bit. You don't have to like it – your challenge is just to keep an open mind and stick with it.

> **True**
> 'Sometimes the questions are complicated and the answers are simple.'
> Dr Seuss

In almost all the difficult areas of your life, you are the problem and the solution. You are a walking talking spaghetti junction of a belief system. 'I can't do it', 'Life is hard', 'Life is unfair', 'Something will go wrong', 'I'm not qualified enough', 'I'm too qualified', 'I hate my hips', 'I'll get found out', 'I can't dance' ...

Ideas and beliefs are imprinted on you. So, you start as a blank slate and then, with continued repetition and some modelling of the people around you, you developed a way of thinking and a set of beliefs. Earlier, I suggested your self-image is a belief. I'm called 'Andrew' because that's what my mum and dad said my name was and it's an idea that has stuck with me for 49 years. And other stuff was added that has imprinted on my subconscious to the point that I've become who I *think* I am. I believe it and live up (or sometimes down) to it.

. NEWS FLASH .

you are not a cucumber!

So, this section is an attempt to unpick some of these beliefs and delve into what makes us human. Starting with the basics, you are not a cucumber. As well as being a bit of a relief, this is also a reminder that a cucumber seed will only ever turn into one thing. In the same way that a rose will only ever be a rose and a banana will only ever succeed in being a banana, these things are locked into one reality.

But you have consciousness, which gives you a lot more potential. It can't turn you into a banana, but it gives you the power to think, rationalize, emote, empathize and imagine, all skills that elude your common-or-garden flora and tree frogs.

Before I take a peek under the bonnet at how our out-dated model of thinking lets us down, it's worth exploring the number-one method that humans use to control their mind – willpower. At some point you will have willed yourself to eat less, exercise more, stop smoking or cut down on social media, in which case you will have sussed that willpower involves massive effort. Basically, willpower means that you are battling against your own thinking. Actually, it suggests that you haven't had a true change of heart. You haven't let go. Willpower might raise you from the couch or help you choose salad instead of chips but, if you were truly passionate about getting fit or losing weight, then willpower wouldn't be needed. Your will becomes free.

As soon as the going gets tough ('Mmmm, which one, salad or chips?') willpower collapses. Essentially, you are attempting to cosh your thoughts into submission to the point that 'I really want some chips' gets the heavy treatment. The thought takes a mighty clobbering but it's never killed off – it just lurks, sobbing in the corner of your mind.

> Fact
> If you mistreat your thoughts, they will make you unhappy!
> ...and we wouldn't want that!

At the core of all human behaviour, most people's needs are more or less similar. We want more positive experiences because they make us feel good and they're easy to handle. It's negative experiences that we all struggle with. Therefore, what we get out of life is not determined purely by the good feelings we desire but by what bad feelings we're willing and able to sustain to get us to those good feelings.

For example, if I want a washboard stomach, I know that I will have to endure the pain, time and effort of spending hours in the gym. And the clincher is that I might have to drink less beer. So my wanting a six-pack tummy weighs less than my desire for an easy life. Similarly, you want to quit your job and start up your own business but to do so means enduring financial uncertainty, risk and long hours.

So, counterintuitively, the question may be less about what you want to achieve and more like 'What pain are you willing to sustain to achieve it?' What if, paradoxically, the quality of your life is not determined by the quality of your positive experiences but your willingness to tolerate negative experiences?

'If you're caught in a trap, what's the one thing you have to do before you can escape? You have to realize that you've been caught in a trap!'

Jamie Smart

Curiouser and Curiouser

what the heck are they? Thoughts

Thoughts – what the heck are they? I mean, have you ever stopped to consider not only what they are but are we 'experiencing' them or 'doing' them?

Thought not!

Here's a fact: thoughts aren't facts. They're not real things. If we're 'experiencing' them, it would suggest that they're coming whether we want them or not, and we have very little control over what's coming. If we're 'doing' them, then we are the creator and the experiencer.

Your life isn't actually real. It's created by thought. These sentences send you down Alice in Wonderland's rabbit hole of consciousness into the netherworld of weirdness. At the bottom lies the question: 'While you are busy thinking, who's the one *noticing* that you're thinking?'

If your thoughts create your reality, you are only ever one thought away from creating an entirely different experience of being alive. Most of us go through our waking hours taking little notice of our thought processes. It's safe to say that how the mind goes about its business never crosses your mind. What it fears, what it says to itself, what it notices and what it doesn't notice – for the most part, we go through life thinking but paying minimal attention to *how* we think.

Strap yourself in for some uncomfortable stuff. Consciousness – what the heck is it? There's a physical you, but there's another you, experiencing the physical you. The flesh-and-blood you allows your consciousness to get around town. The 'you' you see in the mirror is just a means of transport.

Hold on to something or somebody – we're going deep. Your brain has no access to the outside world. It's locked away in a dark and silent box, called a skull. Your brain can't see, hear, touch, smell or taste. Your senses detect stimuli 'out there' and translate them into a language that the brain can understand. So sight, hearing, touch, smell and taste aren't real – they are an electrochemical rendition in a dark theatre.

Here's an example: let's assume you are looking at a bumblebee buzzing around some flowers. First up, and rather disturbingly, the bee's colour doesn't really exist. Nor does its sound. Yes, the bee is there. It's a 'thing', emitting electromagnetic radiation and sound waves, but it's only inside your head that this becomes yellow and black and buzzing. We believe our image of the bee to be real, but it's entirely constructed from inside the sealed container. We could do the same with smell. Disturbingly, reality is odourless; there's no such thing as 'smell' outside our brains. 'Smell' is a bunch of molecules floating about in the air that your nose receptors process and turn into what we call a 'smell'.

So, unless you're incredibly enlightened, you will have fallen for that classic schoolboy error of thinking reality is real. And now you're chuckling to yourself – 'Andy, now you've explained it so well, how could I have not seen it before? It's soooo obvious! All along I've been "constructing" my reality. I feel such a fool!'

You're not thinking that at all, are you? More likely you're thinking it's airy-fairy new-age quantum physics law-of-attraction mumbo-jumbo and imagining that I must be decked out in sandals, socks, linen trousers and a hemp shirt. And, in a deliciously serendipitous way, you will give up on this chapter, thereby letting your thinking win.

Hang in there, because these next couple of sentences are a tad confusing but very important. Because, you see, *attention* is a finite resource. There are so many stimuli out there that you cannot attend to everything that happens so you make choices of what to attend to and, quite simply, these choices create your reality. The vast majority of these choices are made on autopilot, underneath the radar of your conscious mind.

Let's cut to someone with massive credibility, *Professor Paul Dolan*, who took an entire book to say just one thing: your happiness is determined by how you allocate your attention. After ploughing through *Happiness by Design: Change What You Do, Not How You Think* (Penguin, 2015) and gleaning this one thing, it's tempting to snap the book shut and yell, 'You're a professor for goodness' sake! Is that it? Is that all you've got to tell me? You've taken a whole book to tell me THAT?'

But on reflection you will figure out what I have figured out, that this *one thing* is the glue that holds your life together. One thing, your attention, is what creates your reality. And, although your attention may be on something out there, the focus creates thinking 'in here' (picture me, tapping the side of my head).

Quote

'What information consumes is rather obvious: it consumes the attention of its recipients.'

Herbert Simon

Dolan's rather fabulous point is that there are warehouses stocked full of research about what inputs you need to have in order to produce the output of happiness. So, for example, maybe there's a certain income level that will make you happy. Or an amount of bling. Or a particular type of job. Or a precise quaffing of alcohol. Or an optimum number of marriages.

Dolan recasts the inputs as stimuli vying for your attention. The effect of income on happiness therefore becomes less about the actual amount you earn and more about how much attention you're giving the thought. He argues that we're in the 'attention economy'; we are bombarded with information so our heads are screaming about which bits to focus our thoughts on. The point being your choice of focus becomes your reality.

Maureen Gaffney (*doctor and clinical psychologist,* no less) makes the same point, describing attention as the gateway between us and the world around us, between the event happening to us and the event happening *within* us. So how we direct our thinking and attention becomes crucial in creating our reality.[65]

You have twigged why diamonds and gold are so expensive – they are finite resources where demand exceeds supply. Much the same applies to your 'attention'. And because there is not enough of it to go around, it becomes an incredibly precious individual and organizational asset.

Bluntly, what you pay attention to becomes your life. Both academics are suggesting that attention is your psychological currency so you should spend it wisely!

Without even realizing it, we've been using an old model of thinking and attempting to transpose it on to the new world. This misunderstanding gives rise to massive stress and overthinking that clouds our awesomeness.

Made Andy pretty angry!

The prevailing model of human nomenclature is that what happens on the outside determines our experience on the inside. After all, we all know that other people can 'make' us happy or angry. And when I forgot to pay my London Congestion Charge and it cost me £120 I was angry. I mean, the injustice of it! It's not just me, we're built that way, or if I was being super-insightful I'd say that we're designed to be fooled that way.

Immanuel Kant's theory of idealism suggests that our eyes don't transmit the world to us but, rather, we see a combination of what our eyes see with what we already think, know, feel and want to believe. It uses this combination of sensory information and pre-existing experience to construct our perception of reality. So, hold on, aren't we back to that nagging suspicion that 'reality' isn't real? That it's *constructed*? Kant wrote, 'The understanding can intuit nothing, the sense can think nothing. Only through their union can knowledge arise.'[66]

Dan Gilbert describes it brilliantly: 'We feel as though we are sitting comfortably inside our heads, looking out through the clear glass windows of our eyes, watching the world as it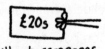

Gilbert compares it to fake £20s

truly is.'[67] But we're actually not. Instead, our brains are foraging for information to weave into our memory and perception to create a view of the world whose detail is so compelling that we never question it. Gilbert's analogy is to imagine you are a counterfeiter, producing £20 notes. You are also acting as the victim. You are the producer of fake £20 notes and passing them off to yourself, without even holding them up to the light.

I must hold up my hands at this point. I continue to struggle with this in its purest form. There's a sort of Zen black belt of counterfeit thinking that makes sense at a purely academic level, but which, for me, sometimes falls at the first hurdle. I've been working hard at catching glimpses of this so-called illusion. No matter how scary or traumatic your experience of life may be, the idea is to realize that it's only your own thinking that you're experiencing and, with that realization, that self-same 'thinking' should lose much of its hold on you. You may still experience horrible feelings but, once you realize that they're caused by what's inside you, you don't feel compelled to change the world in order to feel good. You have to change you.

And, dear reader, that can sound very harsh indeed.

Not-so-vicious Syd

There is a multitude of personal development, spiritual and business books offering a recipe for a better, slimmer, fitter, happier, richer, more positive, popular, confident you. I'm addicted and, in fact, struggle to get through the day without some sort of self-help fix. So I have ended up being a bit of a self-help nerd, a know-all, possibly even a bit of a personal development smart-arse. And, just occasionally, along creeps something that piques my interest. It's not 'new' exactly, but written in such a way that makes me go 'Wow!'

With that in mind I give you 'inside–out thinking'.

There's a big fat chance that you've never heard of Sydney Banks. I'm not saying that Syd's the messiah. Sure, he had a beard and occasionally wore sandals, but Syd had fewer followers and was a welder who worked in the Glasgow shipyards. Syd based the last 20 years of his life espousing that we fall into the trap of thinking that our feelings are telling us about our life whereas in actual fact your feelings are telling you about your thinking.

The icing on the philosophical cake is that your thinking might not even be, strictly speaking, yours. It's up there with the best of Buddhism but, to be fair to Syd, he didn't know about any of this background stuff – he just had an epiphany. Imagine, one day he's sitting on deck, riveting two pieces of steel together on a new cruise-liner and the next minute it's WHAM, he has an epiphany that tells him human beings are gifted with creating their own reality.

That's one helluva day at the office! (In fact, riveting in all senses of the word.)

There are some fabulous books that have attempted to unpick Syd's work and bring it to the masses. Jack Pransky's[68] books articulate it brilliantly. Jamie Smart's[69] and Michael Neill's[70] are both recent, relevant and highly recommended. Elsie Spittle was a friend of Syd's so she has it from the horse's mouth, so to speak.[71]

Before I give my take on inside–out thinking, I am at pains to acknowledge that I come from a position of a mind cluttered by my research. The academic process has taught me to be critical and to look for evidence. I feel like a foie-gras goose, force-fed a diet of journals and heavyweight texts that often have to be read and re-read three or four times before they become remotely fathomable. And here we have something so simple, academically unproven and from the shallow end of 'easy' that chimes with everything I've learned. If you marry the two, then you get an explosion of what I'll call 'unacademic enlightenment'.

Best of all, what if it doesn't need proving in a laboratory? What if it just works?

'The GREATEST obstacle to DISCOVERY is NOT ignorance — it is the illusion of KNOWLEDGE'

Dan Boorstin

Syd's epiphany lay in knowing that it's your thoughts that create your reality and, thus, you can stop the search for happiness. His insight that it's all an inner journey is both its joy and its downfall. On the one hand, it's a blessed relief to learn that I don't have to do any more learning or read any more books. All I have to learn about is me. But, on the other hand, there's the realization that I'm the most complicated thing in the universe.

The inside–out revolution's first insight is that your thoughts create your feelings. So, for example, it's not the £120 London Congestion Charge fine that's making me angry. The event is neutral. That 'incident' means absolutely nothing until I attach some thinking to it – 'The greedy corporate bastards!' – which in turn releases a gush of feelings. I am therefore the creator of my own experience. This simple realization is transformational in its own right. But its simplicity might also be its downfall. You don't have to be clever. You don't need to have a Ph.D. in anything to get this. In fact, I have a nagging suspicion that it helps if you haven't.

An awesome version of you is much closer than you think...

I'd class it as an insight rather than a theory. Once you stop critically evaluating, excuse the lack of academic evidence and just go with the flow, it can burst open the door of your belief system and expose the fact that there's an awesome version of you much closer than you think. What a cunning hiding place – *inside your head!* Think *The Shining* but without the chill-factor. Instead of Johnny peering menacingly through the door, replace Jack

Nicholson's face with a beaming one that's saying 'Here's insight!'

Let me simplify what is already a simple concept: your thinking is the source of your feelings. But hang on, that turns your entire filing cabinet of lifelong learning on its head. Until now, you unquestionably imagined that external events created your feelings. The £120 fine that I've just this minute gone online and paid, that's what made me angry. Or the miserable weather outside my window, that's what made me feel dreary. Or the heated argument with my teenage daughter, that's what made me irritated. Most people will sail through life reacting to external events, totally oblivious to the level of insight to which this chapter has taken you.

So if we delve a little deeper, what Syd Banks espoused is not that the world is influenced by thought to the extent that we can manipulate our thoughts towards the positive and therefore feel a bit better. *No siree*. Syd's notion is that the entire word is generated *from* thought.

Ready for the simplest piece of philosophy ever? You'd probably best be sitting down. Here it is...

It's not what you think, it's that YOU are the thinker.

Ta-da! Now if you're anything like me, you'll have already figured that you are the thinker. In fact, you will have twigged that you are a thinking machine with that little voice in your head that does the running commentary throughout the day. Most people think nice and quietly in their head but some think aloud, wandering around at work muttering to themselves: 'I think I'll have a jacket tatty for my tea but what to have on it? Cheese or beans?'

Either way, that's thinking, albeit of the trivial kind. Most people never go any further than realizing *that* they think. They might play around with giving themselves a pep talk when times are tough, or putting a positive spin on a rainy day ('It's good for the garden') or maybe, as I argued earlier, they chuck in a bit of willpower. That's normal.

The realization that your emotions stem from your thinking (and absolutely nothing else) is a major next step. So it isn't the event (e.g. the rainy day) that's causing you to be feel glum, it's your thinking about the rainy day. Tinkering with the content of your thoughts ('It's good for the garden') will give you a temporary emotional uplift. Once again, that's as far as most people venture. Realizing that your feelings are just a thought means that you can let that thought pass and catch on to another more uplifting one that's sure to be on the way.

So, let's tackle the naysayers right at the beginning: 'If I create my reality, I'd be creating a better one than the blandness my life is right now.' No kid gloves here, folks. And my answer is a rather brusque: 'Yes, you would. So do it.'

Thinking is a good thing. Or, at least, it can be! But if you spend all your time cursing about the injustice of your £120 fine, your thinking will be draining you. Your mind has a pipeline of thought. It can be like a Victorian sewage pipeline, clogged with shit. Or it can be a fresh, clean pipeline, flowing with a gentle stream of positivity and appreciation.

Of course, there are times in everyone's life when the past rears its beastly head and a rush of negativity floods over you. Or someone treats you horribly and you go off on one. 'Inside-out' thinking at ninja level will stop that. But I'm nowhere near ninja level and I don't think the human being is necessarily designed to know this stuff. We're built for 'outside–in' thinking. We anticipate and react. That's what we've always done and we've evolved into higher-order species through doing it. This new-fangled 'inside–out' thinking is almost like thinking on steroids. It's cheating. It gives you an unfair advantage over the rest of life's runners and riders who are thinking in the old way. Inside–out thinking won't make everything rosy but is will prevent you from taking negative thoughts, even ones that seem viciously real, too seriously for too long. It's perhaps not cheating in the Lance Armstrong way. It's far more enlightened than that. As life unfolds in an alpine-like uphill climb, inside–out thinking should enable you to power ahead.

If Syd was correct, it's reassuring to know that, whatever your past or present situations, you are only ever one thought away from happiness. This remarkable ability is available to everyone but most are totally unaware of it. It costs nothing and no talent or qualifications are required – just a bit of insight and, from my experience, quite a lot of practice.

But there's always a flipside. If I accept the notion that happiness is only one thought away, I must also accept that so, too, are sadness, anger, frustration, jealousy and rage. Mentioning the £120 for a fifth time begins to feel like minor post-traumatic stress disorder, so I shall take my own medicine and stop thinking about it.

Can it really be that easy? The very short answer is 'yes'. The slightly longer answer follows.

Why NOW is a good place to start

Syd Banks never knew it but he was remarkably in tune with the better-known Eckhart Tolle. If you're going to stick your head into *The Power of Now: A Guide to Spiritual Enlightenment* (Yellow Kite, 2001), I'd recommend you look away now because here's a plot spoiler – you might be putting your happiness in the wrong time zone.

Tolle, in line with the best mindfulness tradition, says that all you have is 'now'. In fact, life is nothing but a series of nows. Leaving aside the terrifying notion of how many 'nows' have passed you by because you've been too busy focusing on the past or the future, Tolle's point is that there is no 'past' or 'future' as such. Everything you ever experience is experienced through the lens of now. So all the fabulous stuff you've done in the past can only be remembered as you are now. And your future can be imagined only from the point of now. The past and present can be comprehended only in this moment of thought. They don't exist anywhere else.

Gulp!

If you delve a bit further, to suffer the past you have to remember the past now and create bad feelings in the present. Your bad feelings aren't stored anywhere. There's not some bottomless well of sorrow that you can tap into or, conversely, an unbridled spring of joy. It's all

accessible through thought and absolutely nowhere else.
'Now where did I put that depressed feeling? Oh yes, in
1983 when my first husband cheated on me, the bastard!'
and off you go – one thought and you've jumped into a
self-created well of rage.

The incident happened in 1983 and one thought can take
you back there. But you can only get back there through
the wormhole of *now*.

Lessons from the boyz

Having spent ten years as a researcher, I'd describe
myself as a recovering academic. The journals and
papers spat out by the higher-education system can be
unfathomable to the masses, a peer group whom I am
very much part of. I have a Ph.D. but I'm not very clever. I
achieved it through hard graft, sacrifice of family time and
sheer bloody-mindedness. I suspect this might be why I
have more than a passing admiration for Syd Banks. He
wasn't pretending to be clever either.

So let's introduce someone who is:
a German scientist by the name of
Jakob von Uexküll.[72] Immediately there
are three ingredients that prove his

German ⎫
Scientist ⎬ Prove
Silly name ⎭ intelligence

intelligence: he's 'German' and a scientist and has a silly
name. Uexküll suggested the part of the world we can
see and be aware of is called the *Umwelt* (which is simply
the German word for 'environment'). Essentially, that's
your world, the one you can see, hear, touch, taste and
smell. Each species has its own *Umwelt*, its own little
world that it knows but outside of which lives an entire
earthly universe that it never considers. For example, I
have two pet pigs (affectionately known as 'my boyz' –
yes, with a 'z') who live in a piggy world. They are totally
tuned in to food to the point that they have evolved with

The boyz

snouts that are low to the ground and beady eyes that can see close up, perfect for foraging for apples that have fallen from the trees. They know they live in a pig pen and, if I let them out of their field, they know where the apple trees are. They are clever animals but I doubt either of them knows about the FTSE 100 or that just one mile away there is a Sainsbury's supermarket. Both pigs accept their *Umwelt* and stop there. They unquestioningly accept reality as it is presented to them. As do you. Your *Umwelt* is (hopefully) bigger than my boyz's. You, at least, will suss that there's a Sainsbury's in town or, if not, you would be able to Google it (in fairness to my boyz, that's difficult if you have trotters).

Now here's where it gets interesting. Outside of your conscious world lies what Uexküll calls your *Umgebung*. As well as being a fabulous word, it's also a superb concept. This is the world beyond your *Umwelt* – thoughts and experiences that have never even made it to the front door of your consciousness, never mind having rung the bell to be let in. Donald Rumsfeld famously tripped over himself with this description of the *Umwelt*: 'There are known knowns. These are things we know that we know. There are known unknowns. That is to say, there are things that we know we don't know. But there are also unknown unknowns. There are things we don't know we don't know.'

My research throws two very big factors into play. A positive mindset is largely a choice and that choice requires effort. So, the Ph.D. thinking goes, it takes effort to be positive and, because there's a modicum of effort involved, most people will default to the path of least resistance, which is to grumble and whinge their way through life, fitting into the far easier social norm of attitudinal mediocrity. Remember, we're programmed to respond to danger so the negative thoughts are shouting louder. *Pick me, pick me ...*

If you look at inside–out thinking, the choice bit remains strong but the 'effort' bit dies. It's therefore quite a relief to find that we don't have to try to improve ourselves or try to do better. Once we realize that we are the creator of our thoughts it's like lighting the pilot light of inspiration and *whoosh* – your fire burns brighter and you change for the better. It's instant and effortless. So, following the analogy, the potential to go whoosh is always there. Everyone's internal pilot light is lit, but not everybody's boiler gets to ignite.

All of this is a bit weird, or at least it is for me. And, despite knowing what I know, both academically and non-academically, and despite its apparent simplicity, I still sometimes struggle to grasp the concept. How can it be that something so simple remains so difficult? I figured out long ago that 'simple' isn't the same as 'easy'. How is it that I can sometimes forget that I have this so-called inner wisdom? And yet, other days, I'm glowing like it's the most obvious thing in the world? And why did I not know this before? And why on earth wasn't I taught it at school? And how come I keep forgetting? Am I doing something wrong?

When you catch on to the illuminating insight that our thinking creates our reality, it's tempting to tinker with our thoughts. You end up analysing your thinking, challenging it and working to swap negative thoughts for positive ones. The weird bit for me is to go with Syd's idea that just realizing that it's thought is enough. That's where the purity lies. But it's easy to fall into the quicksand of figuring why and what you're thinking. So the inside–out way says that if you feel angry you are best to acknowledge that it's a result of your thinking. That realization in itself is more likely to bring clarity than attempting to override your feeling.

The big question for me is this: should we seek to tinker with our thinking and corral it towards the positive as and when? Personally, I feel there's significant value in being able to do that. That's what 'talking therapies' such as CBT attempt to do. Syd's notion was that we don't have to do anything other than allow healthier thoughts to emerge and that wellbeing is our default setting. I understand the insightful nature of what he's saying. I get it on a theoretical level. It's just that my life isn't lived at theoretical level; it's insanely and relentlessly practical.

I have a lot of time for Syd's work. But I think there's also some serious mileage in Richard Wilkins's concept of Broadband Consciousness (BC). He's rather like Syd in that what he says isn't backed by reams of academic papers – it doesn't need to be – it just works. Unlike Syd, Richard has that rare pleasure of being alive. In fact, extremely alive! Going on a BC workshop is like being plugged back into the mains!

A distinct possibility

'Your greatest frustration isn't that you don't know what to do – it's knowing exactly what to do and still not doing it.'

Richard Wilkins

So what is BC and how does it tally with inside–out thinking? Richard's notion is that everyone has a script – the running commentary in your head, commonly known as your thinking. Your script is an accumulation of life experiences and you play to it. You think it's you and you believe everything it says. So, for example, I recently met a 15-year-old lad who was a whisker away from being excluded from school. His script was telling him that he was from a broken home, fitted into a gang and didn't need school, so mucking about and being disrespectful to teachers was fine. That's the role he was playing. Richard's concept of BC suggests that you cannot change the script. It's written, so you can't rewrite it. What you can do is to understand that it's just a script. It's your *Umwelt*. You've learned it word for word. So acknowledging it as such means that you can step out of the script. In the lad's example, he can keep doing what his script is telling him or he can recognize it as a script and step outside of it. The realization that you are reading from a script gives you a whole load of options that you wouldn't otherwise have.

Of course, trying to do nothing is doing something, so if you're not careful you can get caught in some sort of paradox. I spent the first 40 years of my life living down to my script. And then I had a realization, bordering on an epiphany, and it was this: that if I waited for everyone else to be inspired, I'd die waiting, so I might as well focus on the only person I could do anything about – *me!* So the revolution began, *in my head.* The only way I knew of instilling the principles in other people was to instil them in me first.

I know that may sound naive and simplistic, almost a copout perhaps, but I can't force anyone else to be positive or happy. But, by adopting the ideas myself, I will have some sort of impact; plus, it may evoke a bit of curiosity in others.

So I was no longer trying to 'convert' people to happiness, I was sharing. The best 'sharing' is living what I know, which for me is from a state of gratitude where I see life as a gift. As I have changed, miraculous events have naturally unfurled around me, my relationships have strengthened and my interactions with others have changed for the better. I have indeed been 'born again', just not in *that* way.

So, in my opinion, Richard Wilkins and Syd Banks should

be knighted, for 'services to the common people – cutting through the crap and telling us how it really is'.

You are the source

Ready for a mighty clash of academic and non-academic thinking that is my very own 'Big Bang' theory?

Mindfulness and inside–out thinking teach us that consciousness is a river of never-ending thoughts and that we have to recognize that thoughts are just thoughts and keep watching them float by until a good one comes along. A bit like the 1980s computer game Frogger.

'We shape clay into a pot, but it is the emptiness inside that holds whatever we want.'

Lao Tzu

The conundrum comes from the insight that *what* we think about is less important than the fact *that* we think. You have to roll that one around your head (serendipitously, you have to think about it!) a couple of times before it makes any sense. It's less about the intellectual exploration of which thought is causing what emotion and more of a realization that thoughts are always floating by and you can choose to bring your attention to whichever ones you fancy.

Of course, some thoughts scream and yell for attention as they pass by. Sometimes it's hard to let these ones simply float away; they're shaking their fist and shouting louder as they sail past. 'Hey, you, it was an injustice that you were made redundant five years ago. It was your manager's fault. What a bastard she was.' Jump aboard that thought and before you know it, you're back in the emotional quagmire of five years ago. It's comforting (but also slightly unnerving) to know that you don't have to do anything other than allow healthier thoughts to emerge.

Choosing to be positive is not really 'positive thinking'. It's much bigger than that. It's about being at the source end of the river of consciousness.

The realization is that consciousness is an endless stream of thoughts, but it's your stream. If there are more positive thoughts flowing by, you enjoy massively enhanced odds of picking one.

I've ended up doing ten years of research that proves Syd Banks and Richard Wilkins are spot on. Academia works in slow and mysterious ways as if sometimes it takes time for intellect to catch up with insight.

Chapter 8
Genetic intelligence

In the interests of helping you recover from Chapter 7, this one is much shorter. But please don't confuse 'short' with 'small' – the themes are massive! We move swiftly from a Hungarian medic to how you morphed from a single-cell zygote into a 70-trillion-piece genetic jigsaw.

I introduce the most amazing science that you've never heard of – epigenetics – via some balls atop a hill. Here's a question you've never been asked before: how does a liver cell decide to be a liver cell? Why didn't it decide, for example, to be an eye cell? I'm not entirely sure we actually answer that one, but the suggestion is that the outside world is an 'experience' but it also has physical effects. If you 'get it', this chapter will spark some thinking that will stay with you long after you've finished the book.

And, finally, your mission (should you choose to accept it) is to find your mission. Top tip: make it a worthwhile one.

Interesting notion
'No one can go back and make a brand-new start but anyone can start from now and make a brand-new ending.'
Carl Bard

Bonkers ideas

It's a little embarrassing that after ten years of hard study, the best advice I can give people is to exercise their choice to be positive! The conscious choice to be positive of thought and action seems so intuitively obvious that most people don't see it.

So, life-changing though the choice thing is, I'd better see if I can offer you something more amazing. Remember, the choice to be positive and the associated effort of doing so is not my theory, it comes from nigh-on ten years of research into happy people. I've followed them around, almost stalking them in my quest to find the secret of happiness. And I've written my findings in painstaking detail, running to 100,000 words of paint-dryingly turgid academia.

And what if I (and they) are completely wrong? What if we replaced 'choice' and 'effort' with 'awareness' and 'ease'? And what if traditional therapy is almost exactly wrong? That would be a very brave chapter to write. Well, brace yourself, because here it comes ...

Let's look at the story of Ignaz Semmelweis, a Hungarian medic, circa a lot of years ago, who had the bonkers idea that washing your hands before performing surgery would stop people dying. Because, at the time (as recently as the mid-nineteenth century), the thinking was that people got ill from smells. So, if you had a fever, your mum would put a nice vase of fresh flowers in your room, to take away the stench and to make sure your smell didn't infect the family. So Ignaz's theory that these invisible germ thingies were killing people was, well, laughable. It's a sad story because they banged the poor bloke up in an asylum

19th century thinking

Some flowers will make ya better!

and, get this, he died of septicaemia at age 47, which, in a macabre twist of irony, could have been avoided if the doctors had just washed their hands.

So, beliefs change! What was laughable back in the day might come and bite you on the bum. When I'm scraggy haired, long bearded and banged up in some sort of institution, babbling about thought, consciousness and epigenetics, please stand by me. I might not be quite as crazy as I seem. But there's an equal chance that I might be, so you're probably best not to visit me alone.

Gene therapy

This isn't going to sound very romantic but, physically, you are nothing more than a squelching cauldron of chemicals wrapped up in skin. If you were on a supermarket shelf, you'd have a long and complicated list of ingredients. But you started out, amoeba-like, as a single cell called the zygote. It's a terrifying thought but at some point your mum and dad had sex and as his sperm hit your mum's egg, wham, for a brief second, you were a zygote.

Zygote

it's how me and you started out

Welcome to the watery world of amniotic fluid. This zygote is the earliest version of you and its first job is to split in two. You've immediately doubled in size. Those two cells divide, and those two divide, and so on. And now, guess what, you're 70 trillion cells! That's one of those numbers that the human brain can't really imagine. The point is that there are lots of them and they have to learn to differentiate so that you become human. This is something that you've never considered before but your cells have an in-built sense of what they need to become.

A question that gets me scratching my head is, for example, how a liver cell knows it's going to be a liver cell. If you look at cells through a microscope, a brain cell looks radically different from, say, a gut cell. That's interesting if you consider that every cell started out with exactly the same genetic information. And by exactly, I mean *exactly*. Remember, they are derived from the single-cell zygote.

Think about it. Acorns never grow into willow trees. Baby rabbits never grow into wolves. Apple seeds don't become bananas. Somehow the seeds are programmed. Epigenetics asks the curious question that, if we start off as one cell and then we subdivide billions of times ...*how do the cells know what to be?*

> ### Quote
> 'The most exciting breakthroughs of the twenty-first century will not occur because of technology but because of our expanding concept of what it means to be human.'
> John Naisbitt

If you Google 'John Gurdon', you'll find various descriptions of the conceptual framework. And if you Google 'epigenetics', you will not be able to miss references to Conrad Waddington's epigenetic landscape. You'll get a picture of it – a grainy image of a ball at the top of a hill, kind of like this ...

Adjust your budgie smugglers, dear reader – we're going into the deep end of the gene pool.

This picture represents a massive simplification of epigenetics. The ball represents the single-cell zygote. As various cells begin to differentiate, each cell is like a ball that is rolled down the hill. As you can see, it had various routes that take it to one of the troughs at the bottom. Once the ball has gone as far as it can go, that's pretty much where it will stay. So, unless something amazing happens, that cell is never going to turn into another cell (i.e., it's not going to suddenly jump across to another trough). Similarly, it's not going to roll back up the hill and start again.

So, in cellular terms, once a liver cell has become a liver cell, it's not going to suddenly transform into, say, a kidney cell.

With me? So far so good. Except that John Gurdon proved that it is actually possible to haul cells from the very bottom of the trough right back to the top of the hill. And, get this, if the same cell is rolled down the hill again, it will end up in a different trough. So, for example, a liver cell, if it started out again, wouldn't have to be a liver cell. It could change to a heart cell.[73]

I know what you're thinking? *So effing what?*

DNA is the fundamental information source in each cell. Right?

You will have seen pictures of DNA, long strings of genetic blueprints. Despite its complicated look, DNA is a code and it only has four letters (or bases): A, C, G and T (adenine, cytosine, guanine and thymine). Each cell metaphorically rolls down the hill. Which trough it ends up in depends on a myriad of factors, one of which is upbringing. Remember from the previous chapter, the baby's brains are remarkably unfinished. David

Eagleman suggests that, rather than being 'hardwired', babies are 'live-wired'. Thus, early childhood experiences are extremely important in influencing adult life. So, for example, childhood abuse or neglect increases the likelihood of depression in adult life by a whopping 50 per cent.[74] A poor upbringing means you are also more likely to get eating and/or personality disorders. The fact that these disorders arise because you've been 'psychologically damaged' by your early experiences works, intuitively, as a description.

To clarify, 'psychologically damaged' is usually used as a shorthand term for something happening *to* you. But it doesn't explain the molecular events that underlie it. What happens *within* you? For example, what happens to the brains of abused or neglected children?

If early years' neglect and abuse have changed your thinking and character, the question that epigenetics attempts to answer is, how? Epigenetics hypothesizes that terrible childhood experiences are not just psychologically damaging – they actually affect physical aspects of the brain during key developmental phases. Some cells are switched on and off as a result of the abuse. However, and this is also crucial, not every abused child ends up an unwell adult, so there is a degree of flexibility built into the human system. What if (and it's a very big 'WHAT IF?') genes aren't actually fixed but they can get switched on and off? Wouldn't that change everything?

Let's take the example of cortisol, produced in the adrenal glands that sit atop the kidneys. Cortisol is produced in response to stress. Adults who experienced a stressful childhood still record higher than average levels of cortisol. So, a traumatic experience caused a physical switching on of cortisol and it never got switched off again. These adults are experiencing a gushing tap of overwhelming emotions and it's these physical changes that affect emotions and character in later life.

Nessa Carey says it about as well as anyone: 'We have our set of genes, but those genes can be switched on or switched off, and they can be switched on to higher or lower volume levels depending on the environmental stimuli. And epigenetics is a bit like the volume control on an MP3 player. Your MP3 contains the tracks that you have loaded on to it; the ones you choose to play and how loudly you choose to play them, that's controlled by epigenetics.'[75]

Michael Meany did some famous experiments on rats and how they treat their babies. He found that when mummy rats lick and nurture baby rats, it switches certain genes on.

'It doesn't matter who you are or what you look like, so long as somebody loves you.'

Roald Dahl

So, chances are we're all born with similar switches (genes) but the combination of on/off is determined by early years (very early years as it happens). So the genes we're born with are merely nature's starting pistol. It turns out that the rats who were nurtured, loved and licked turned out to be happy well-adjusted rats who, in turn, licked their own offspring. The rats that weren't loved ended up living sad and rather brief lives.

If you've got this far, I think you can draw your own conclusions.

Draw your own conclusions...

Mission Creep

Interesting starting point
'I put my heart and soul into my work, and have lost my mind in the process.'
Vincent van Gogh

You can't opt out of having a mission. Whether you know or acknowledge it, you've living the mission you've chosen. In fact, reading this book, you're carrying it out, right now. Even the basic existence of eating, sleeping and slouching in front of the TV is a mission, of sorts. You will be on a mission of sloth and ease. As I've been at pains to point out, the key is to choose it dynamically rather than acting it out passively.

There are dozens of ways to engage in personal development. You can watch a TED talk or read a book. A lot of people take the information in, but it ends up as sound bites. I used to know a guy who could recite massive chunks of dialogue from the 1980s TV comedy series *Blackadder*. But he wasn't funny. He'd simply remembered what he'd seen and was a mouthpiece for it. I don't want you to learn this book and be able to quote chunks of it at your next meeting. I want you to read and absorb it, get your thinking working for you, question yourself, gain some insight and maybe even some clarity. If I meet you at an 'Art of Being Brilliant' event, I don't want you to say you read my book and it made you laugh. I want you to tell me what you did, and stuck at. Tell me that you make sure your children and grandchildren know you love them, and how it makes a difference.

The massive thought about epigenetics is this: it seems that your genes aren't quite as fixed as you were led to believe. There are thoughts that you can have and actions that you can take that will radically improve your odds of having a fabulous life. And, if you live a good and loving life, the next generation will too. How powerful is that?

So what would your wake-up call be? What would I have to say to get you to 'do' as well as 'understand'? In our workshops we have a very simple activity:

Imagine the world's going to end one week from today. What would you do with your week?

Nobody has ever said: 'I'd just pop into work and clear my in-box.' But there are a lot of people who'd party and tell loved ones that they love them. There are a lot of people who would give a lot of seven-second hugs. And often there's the realization that they don't have to wait until there's just one week left. You could put this book down and hug someone right now.

Some people get a wake-up call, in the form of a breakthrough in their thinking, a major illness or the death of close friend, often someone who was far too young to die. And that really can make people think differently. Your wake-up call can come at any time, or, indeed, not at all. It's quite profound to imagine what your wake-up call might be. What would have to happen for a massive internal alarm bell to shake you from your torpor? And the trick is to appreciate the call came when it did. Don't be embarrassed that you slept in.

Whatever age you are now, wakey-wakey, rise and shine!

There's an element of courage involved in waking up. Most people will be living an ordinary existence that is perfectly fine. For them, that is. But 'ordinary' means long stretches of work and stress followed by short bursts of holiday happiness. Before you know it, we've come full circle to *The Sixth Sense*'s 'I see dead people'.

Epigenetics is screaming for you to use your head. Choose aliveness and pass it on! The brave may not live for ever, but the cautious do not live at all.

Chapter 9

Intelligent futures

A short but razor-sharp finale that starts with a cool story about outsourcing stress. In a celeb-fest of a chapter we introduce quotes from John Lennon, Dolly Parton and Sir Michael Caine.

Life is likened to a massive DIY project and the source of all wisdom is hidden in a sentence that, to be fair, probably should have had some flashing lights or dancing girls so you knew where it was. Look closely now.

And no book is complete without Tarzan and the lessons he taught us about struggling.

The final, final thought attempts to work out the odds of a revolution. Hmm ... where and with whom should it start?

From someone who knew

'When I was five years old my mother told me that happiness was the key to life. When I went to school they asked me what I wanted to be when I grew up. I wrote down "happy". They told me I didn't understand the assignment and I told them they didn't understand life.'

John Lennon

Esquire magazine's editor, 'A. J.' Jacobs, was so busy that he needed a personal assistant. He offloaded all the mundane stuff to start with and, once they'd mastered that, his PA graduated to manage some assignments he didn't fancy. One day, in a flash of enlightenment, A. J. realized that he was worrying about a big project he was working on so he decided to outsource the worry. Let me be clear: he didn't hand over the project, just the fretting. He asked his assistant whether she would worry about the project for him, thereby releasing him extra time to focus on it in a positive way. She agreed. And every day when he started to ruminate he'd remind himself that his PA was already on the case and he'd relax.[76]

In a similar way, I've outsourced the worry of my kids growing up to my wife and delegated all the stress of my business finances to my accountant. As for the stress of worrying whether you enjoy this book or not, well, I've conveniently left that down to you, leaving me fret-free to write a book that makes sense, at least to me.

> What it sometimes feels like
> 'Writing is easy; all you have to do is sit staring at a blank sheet of paper until the drops of blood form on your forehead.'
> Gene Fowler

Dolly Parton once said: 'It takes a lot of money to look this cheap.' Similarly, it's taken a lot of years of learning to make me look 'not particularly clever'. My question at the outset was 'If I was the reader, what would I want to know and how would I want it presented?' The answer is obvious. I'd want a book that challenged my thinking and that rattled my cage (a bit but not too much). I'd also want something that was down to earth, non-pious and was grounded in realism. It might be a bit spiritual but in a non-God way. I'd be keen for a teensy bit of political incorrectness and a big dollop of fun. They're the kinds of books that my personal development heroes write and, if I'm to work on becoming my own superhero, I'd better get cracking on a book that ticks all these boxes. I appreciate that these are my boxes and not necessarily yours.

The temptation was to put the preceding paragraph at the beginning, so you knew what you were getting up-front. You might be a heavyweight academic (not a fat one, a really clever one) who's been tutting and cursing, or a devoutly religious individual who has misinterpreted my lack of godliness as blasphemous. In which case, I apologize for putting you through such anguish. But, for the rest of you, I hope you've enjoyed my simple offering and I have everything crossed that you've learned something along the way.

I am and will always be nothing more than a work in progress.

> ### Quote
> 'I have never seen it. But by all accounts it is terrible. However, I have seen the house that it built and it is terrific.'
> Michael Caine on *Jaws 4*

My final thoughts are about content, style and substance. You will have twigged that *The Little Book of Emotional Intelligence* is neither 'little' nor purely about 'emotional intelligence'. I'm hoping you view it as I do, BIG in size and scope.

I could have played this book with a straight academic bat and it would have been a bit boring but I'd like to think the content would have stood up. Or I could have side-lined the big thoughts and played it for pure comedy. That would have worked too, but for a different audience.

But, on reflection, I am neither particularly clever nor funny. I have done my best to write up some ideas in the only way I know how, in the faint hope that this book reflects your life's project. Because that's what life is, the biggest DIY project ever.

You can sit there and wait for life to pan out as per your dreams, and it pretty much won't. Just as that bedroom won't get painted while you sit looking at it, that awesome life won't get kick-started without some action. And it's the 'effort' bit that puts most people off. The effort comes in a double whammy of having to learn new habits of thinking while simultaneously doing whammy two – giving up old habits.

That second part is what trips people up. You see, it's fairly easy to get things into your head and, once they're lodged, it's very difficult to get them out again.

We're seeking out good feelings. Rhonda Byrne's blockbusting book *The Secret* suggests, Beach Boys style, that they might in fact be 'good vibrations'. So, effectively, you seek a partner not because you need a partner – you want the feeling of love. And, in the same way, you want a job because it makes you feel secure. You want a glass of wine because it makes you feel relaxed. And you don't actually want to go to the gym, but it's the best way to keep your body toned, which makes you feel confident. You are chasing the object because it gives you the feeling. It's the same with this book. You didn't really want to spend a tenner on a book; you wanted it to reveal some nuggets of wisdom that will make you feel alive.

So here's the wisdom. Once you're connected with your best self, the feelings are easier to access because what you really need is *you*. (Waddayamean, is this THE sentence? Of course it is! You'll have to imagine the confetti, tooting horns and dancing girls. Maybe you'll need to read it again and add your own effects.)

A light bulb is pretty much useless on its own. It needs plugging in. In the same vein, you need connecting to an energy force and, in case you haven't twigged, that energy force is you. You shine brightest when you're being your best self.

I've articulated the need to struggle. Here are some thoughts that gradually get bigger. Happiness is both easy and supremely difficult. What if the 'struggle' bit is wriggling out of *outside-in*, and into *inside-out* thinking? Or, what if all of this inside-out stuff is easier than you ever imagined and you didn't need to struggle at all? The biggest thought from Syd Banks and Richard Wilkins might be this: that you literally had to stop struggling to set yourself free.

When I was a kid, I remember watching *Tarzan* (the TV series) in which Ron Ely wore his loincloth very well indeed. And, in almost every episode, someone fell in the quicksand. And they'd struggle like hell in the swampy conditions, sinking deeper and deeper. Cheetah (who wasn't a big cat but a chimp – stay with me, folks) would throw his arms about and scream his concern. Tarzan would translate, telling the person to stop struggling. It seems that the act of struggling was actually sinking them deeper. So, now up to their necks in gunge, they'd attempt to stop struggling and Tarzan would throw them a vine, which they'd grip with their teeth and our hero would haul them out ... unless they were a baddie, in which case they'd keep struggling and go under. My goodness, the 1970s was so exciting!

But it could be that Tarzan's escapades were teaching us a fabulous lesson. There's a lot of metaphorical waving our arms, histrionics and bemoaning our lot and all we seem to be doing is sinking deeper and deeper into the mire of life. So you can do one of two things. Stop falling into life's swamps is a pretty cool top tip. Or, when you inevitably do, stop struggling.

What are the odds?

Top tip: do the lottery. After all, 40,000,000:1 represents such terrific odds if you compare it against the odds of you being here at all.

Do the lottery! ———✳ lotto 123456

Mel Robbins reckons 1 in 400 trillion but I'm not so sure. The statistics start fairly simply with the chances of your mum meeting your dad. And then the chances of them having that first kiss, and an awkward fumble. And the chances of that sperm meeting that egg and you becoming a zygote. But, hang on, you need to factor in the chances of your grandparents meeting and doing the same. And back through your lineage to whoever started the whole shebang. Depending on which belief system you adhere to, the chances are you'd have to trace it all the way back to Eve and Adam or us emerging gills flapping from the marshes. I think Ali Binazir's calculation of 1 in $10^{2,685,000}$ is more like it. But, hang on, it's vastly more complicated than that.

We are a tiny pinprick of life on a speck of solar dust, drifting among billions of other specks. Factor in the odds of our lump of rock spinning off into the Solar System after the Big Bang and then developing the right amount of gravity and water, not to mention a breathable atmosphere. And for our ball of rock to be in the Goldilocks zone of not too near and not too far from the Sun that allows life to flourish at all. I am non-religious (I describe myself as 'not for prophet') but I can't help marvelling at the odds and wondering, somewhere deep in my God Spot, that we must have had some sort of helping hand.

But wondering aside, it's almost infinitesimal odds that you exist at all. We have 28,000 days, which is, in itself, a terrifyingly insignificant fraction of the universe's 14 billion years. This can make you feel so insignificant that you may wonder what's the point. Or it can be hugely liberating. It can release you from the shackles of self-importance. If the gravity of 'life' is weighing on your shoulders heavier than actual gravity, why not go for it? Whatever 'it' ends up being.

My ego is such that I imagine other people will be inspired to take the ideas in this book and investigate further. Was Andy right or can we prove him to be a purveyor of self-help snake-oil? It'd be great if there were some spinoff books that arise, ideally from people who grasp this better than I. Or who are better with words. Maybe someone who can properly explain epigenetics in a way that we can all understand.

There's definitely a story that needs telling and a word that needs spreading. The revolution has started.

No pressure, but if you've got as far as this, it's started with you ...

The revolution has started with you ⟶

NOTES

Chapter 1

1 David Hare, *The Buddha in Me, the Buddha in You: A Handbook for Happiness* (Rider, 2016).

2 http://www.gallup.com/poll/184046/smartphone-owners-check-phone-least-hourly.aspx (2015).

3 T. Buser and N. Peter, 'Multitasking', *Experimental Economics* 15/4 (2012): 1–15.

4 Tony Crabbe, *Busy: How to Thrive in a World of Too Much* (Piatkus, 2015).

5 Robert Holden, *Success Intelligence: Timeless Wisdom for a Manic Society* (Hodder, 2005).

6 Research by the British Psychological Society, reported in *Science Daily*, 11 September 2015. www.sciencedaily.com/releases/2015/09/150911094917.htm

Chapter 4

7 Daniel Goleman, *Emotional Intelligence: Why It Can Matter More Than IQ* (Bantam, 1995), p. 40.

8 Goleman, *Emotional Intelligence*, p. 47.

9 Barbara Fredrickson, *Positivity: Groundbreaking Research to Release Your Inner Optimist and Thrive* (Oneworld, 2011).

10 E. Diener and W. Tov, 'Culture and Subjective Wellbeing', in S. Kitayama and D. Cohen (eds), *Handbook of Cultural Psychology* (Guildford, 2010).

11 M. Stibich, 'Top 10 Reasons to Smile' available at http://longevity.about.com/od/lifelongbeauty/tp/smiling.htm

12 D. Deeg and R. van Zonneveld, 'Does Happiness Lengthen Life?', in R. Veenhoven (ed.), *How Harmful is Happiness?* (Rotterdam University Press, 1989).

13 B. Fredrickson and M. Tugade, 'What Good Are Positive Emotions in Crises? A Prospective Study of Resilience and Emotions Following the Terrorist Attack on the United States on September 11, 2001', *Journal of Personality and Social Psychology* 84 (2003): 365–76.

14 M. Gervais and D. Wilson, 'The Evolution and Functions of Laughter and Humour: A Synthetic Approach', *Quarterly Review of Biology* 80 (2005): 395–430.

15 F. G. Ashby, A. M. Isen and A. U. Turken, 'A Neuropsychological Theory of Positive Affect and its Influence on Cognition', *Psychological Review* 106 (1999), 529–50.

16 T. Wager, D. Scott and J. Zubieta, 'Placebo Effects on Human Opioid Activity during Pain', *Proceedings of the National Academy of the United States of America* 104 (2007): 11056–61.

17 B. Fredrickson and R. Mancuso, 'The Undoing Effect of Positive Emotions', *Motivation and Emotion* 24 (2000): 237–58.

18 K. Gil and J. Carson, 'Daily Mood and Stress Predict Health Care Use and Work Activity in African American Adults with Sickle Cell Disease', *Health Psychology* 23 (2004): 267–74.

19 L. Richman and L. Kubzansky, 'Positive Emotion and Health:

Going Beyond the Negative', *Health Psychology* 24 (2005): 422–9.

20 W. Bardwell and C. Berry, 'Psychological Correlates of Sleep Apnea', *Journal of Psychomatic Research* 47 (1999): 583–96.

21 Sheldon Cohen, David A. J. Tyrrell and Andrew P. Smith, 'Psychological Stress and Susceptibility to the Common Cold', *New England Journal of Medicine* 325 (1991). Available at http://www.nejm.org/doi/full/10.1056/NEJM199108293250903#t=articleResults

22 Chris Peterson, Steven Maier and Martin E. P. Seligman, *Learned Helplessness: A Theory for the Age of Personal Control* (Oxford University Press, 1993).

Chapter 5

23 http://www.forbes.com/sites/meghanbiro/2014/01/19/happy-employees-hefty-profits/

24 M. Royal and M. Star, 'Hitting the Ground Running: What the World's Most Admired Companies Do to (Re)engage Their Employees', The Hay Group, 2010.

25 R. Feloni, *5 Tips to Create Happier Employees* (Globoforce, 2015). E-book available from: http://www.globoforce.com/resources/features/ebook-5-tips-to-create-happier-employees/

26 Shawn Achor, *The Happiness Advantage: The Seven Principles of Positive Psychology that Fuel Success and Performance at Work* (Virgin Books, 2011).

27 S. Kelner, C. Rivers and K. O'Connell, *Managerial Style as a Behavioural Predictor of Organizational Climate* (Boston: McBer & Company, 1996).

28 Jessica Pryce-Jones, *Happiness at Work: Maximizing Your Psychological Capital for Success* (Wiley-Blackwell, 2010).

29 This research, carried out in 1997, was provided to Daniel Goleman and reported in his 1998 book *Working with Emotional Intelligence*.

30 J. E. Hunter, F. L. and M. K. Judiesch, 'Individual Differences in Output Variability as a Function of Job Complexity', *Journal of Applied Psychology* 75 (1990): 28–42.

31 D. Goleman, *Working with Emotional Intelligence* (Bantam, 1998).

32 Robert Kelley and Janet Caplan, 'How Bell Labs Creates Star Performers', *Harvard Business Review* (July–August 1993), pp. 128–39.

33 Simon Sinek, *Start with Why: How Great Leaders Inspire Everyone to Take Action* (Penguin, 2009).

34 K. S. Cameron and B. Winn, 'Virtuousness in Organizations', in K. Cameron and G. Spreitzer (eds), *The Oxford Handbook of Positive Organizational Scholarship* (Oxford University Press, 2013).

35 G. Spreitzer and S. Sonenshein, 'Positive Deviance and

Extraordinary Organizing', in K. S. Cameron, J. Dutton and R. E. Quinn (eds), *Positive Organizational Scholarship* (Berrett-Koehler, 2003), pp. 207–24.

36 K. S. Cameron, *Positive Leadership: Strategies for Extraordinary Performance* (Berrett-Koehler. 2008).

37 T. W. Britt et al, 'Self-engagement at Work', in C. L. Cooper and D. Nelson (eds), *Positive Organizational Behavior: Accentuating the Positive at Work* (Sage, 2007).

38 Christine L. Porath and Thomas S. Bateman, 'Self-regulation: From Goal Orientation to Job Performance', *Journal of Applied Psychology* 91/1 (January 2006): 185–92.

39 I've rounded these figures up. For the precise details, see M. Losada and E. Heaphy, 'The Role of Positivity and Connectivity in the Performance of Business Teams: A Nonlinear Dynamics Model', *American Behavioural Scientist* 47 (2004): 740–65.

40 K. Cameron, *Practicing Positive Leadership: Tools and Techniques That Create Extraordinary Results* (Berrett-Koehler, 2013).

41 Alex Linley, *Average to A+: Realising Strengths in Yourself and Others* (CAPP Press, 2008), p. 58.

42 Tom Rath, *Strengthsfinder 2.0: A New and Upgraded Edition of the Online Test from Gallup's Now Discover Your Strengths* (Gallup Press, 2007).

43 J. K. Harter, F. L. Schmidt and T. L. Hayes, 'Business-unit-level Relationships between Employee Satisfaction, Employee Engagement and Business Outcomes: A Meta-analysis', *Journal of Applied Psychology* 87 (2002): 268–79.

44 *Corporate Leadership Council, Driving Performance and Retention through Employee Engagement: A Quantitative Analysis of Effective Engagement Strategie*s (Corporate Leadership Council, 2004). Available online: http://www.usc.edu/programs/cwfl/assets/pdf/Employee%20engagement.pdf

Chapter 6

45 David Eagleman, *The Brain: The Story of You* (Canongate, 2015).

46 M. Wolfenstein, 'Fun Morality: An Analysis of Recent American Child-training Literature', in M. Mead and M. Wolfenstein (eds), *Childhood in Contemporary Cultures* (University of Chicago Press, 1955).

47 S. F. Berk, *The Gender Factory: The Apportionment of Work in American Households* (Plenum Press, 1985).

48 M. M. Ferree, 'Beyond Separate Spheres: Feminism and Family Research', *Journal of Marriage and the Family* 52 (1990): 866–84.

49 J. P. Robinson, *How Americans Use Time: A Social–Psychological Analysis of Everyday Behaviour* (Praeger, 1997).

50 J. H. Pleck, 'Men in Domestic Settings: American Fathering in Historical Perspective', in Michael S. Kimmel (ed), *Changing Men* (Sage, 1987), pp. 83–97.

51 E. A. Rotundo, 'American Fatherhood: A Historical Perspective', *American Behavioural Scientist* 29 (1985): 7–27.

52 H. Galdin, 'Child Discipline and the Pursuit of Self: An Historical Interpretation', in Hayne W. Reese and Lewis P. Lipsitt (eds), *Advances in Child Development and Behavior* (Academic Press, 1978), pp. 231–65.

53 W. W. Collins and G. Russell, 'Mother–Child and Father–Child Relationships in Middle Childhood and Adolescence: A Developmental Analysis', *Developmental Review* 11 (1991): 99–136.

54 J. Youniss and J. Smollar, *Adolescent Relations with Mothers, Fathers and Friends* (University of Chicago Press, 1985).

55 R. Larson and R. Richards, *Divergent Realities: The Emotional Lives of Mothers, Fathers and Adolescents* (Basic Books, 1994).

56 T. Parsons, 'Age and Sex in the Social Structure of the United States', *American Sociological Review* 7 (1942): 604–16.

57 A. Collins, 'Parent–Child Relationships in the Transition to Adolescence: Continuity and Change in Interaction, Affect, and

Cognition', in Raymond Montemayor, Gerard R. Adams and Thomas P. Gullotta (eds), *From Childhood to Adolescence: A Transition Period?* (Sage, 1990), pp. 85–106.

58 B. E. Compass et al, 'Parent and Child Stress and Symptoms: An Integrative Analysis', *Developmental Psychology* 25 (1989): 550–9.

59 J. Cassidy et al, 'Family–Peer Connections: The Roles of Emotional Expressiveness within the Family and Children's Understanding of Emotions', *Child Development* 63 (1992): 603–18.

60 S. L. Gable et al, 'What Do You Do When Things Go Right? The Intrapersonal and Interpersonal Benefits of Sharing Positive Events', *Journal of Personality and Social Psychology* 87/2 (2004): 228–45.

61 C. Dweck, *Mindset: How You Can Fulfil Your Potential* (Robinson, 2012).

62 Amit Sood, *Mayo Clinic Handbook for Happiness: A Four-Step Plan for Resilient Living* (Da Capo Lifelong Books, 2015).

63 Alva Noë, *Out of Our Heads: Why You Are Not Your Brain, and Other Lessons from the Biology of Consciousness* (Hill & Wang, 2010).

64 B. Hart and T. Risley, *Meaningful Differences in the Everyday Experience of Young American Children* (Paul H. Brookes Publishing, 1995).

Chapter 7

65 M. Gaffney, *Flourishing* (Penguin, 2012).

66 Immanuel Kant, *The Critique of Pure Reason,* trans. by Norman Kemp Smith (Macmillan, 1929).

67 Gilbert Daniel, *Stumbling on Happiness* (Harper Perennial, 2007).

68 Jack Pransky, S*omebody Should Have Told Us!: Simple Truths for Living Well*, 3rd edn (CCB Publishing, 2011).

69 Jamie Smart, *Clarity Clear Mind, Better Performance, Bigger Result*s (Capstone, 2013).

70 Michael Neill, *The Inside-Out Revolution: The Only Thing You Need to Know to Change Your Life Forever* (Hay House, 2013).

71 Elsie Spittle, *Wisdom or Life: Three Principles for Well-Being* (Lone Pine Publishing, 2005).

72 Carlo Brentari, Jakob von Uexküll, *The Discovery of the Umwelt between Biosemiotics and Theoretical Biolog*y (Springer, 2015).

73 Nessa Carey, *The Epigenetics Revolution: How Modern Biology Is Rewriting Our Understanding of Genetics, Disease and Inheritance* (Icon Books, 2012).

74 C. Heim et al, 'Neurobiological and Psychiatric Consequences of Child Abuse', *Developmental Psychobiology* 52/7 (2010): 671–90.

75 Carey, *The Epigenetics Revolution* (Icon Books, 2012).

Chapter 9

76 Tim Ferris, *The 4-Hour Workweek* (Crown Publishers, 2007).

About us:

  Author: Andy Cope aka Dr HAPPY

Andy describes himself as a qualified teacher, author, happiness expert and learning junkie. He has spent the last 10 years studying positive psychology, happiness & flourishing, culminating in a Loughborough University PhD thesis. He is not a natural academic and has learned to appreciate the delicious irony that his happiness research has, on occasion, made him unhappy.

Andy's research feeds into a series of workshops and keynotes and he's lucky enough to work with organisations such as DHL, Hewlett Packard, Astra Zeneca, Sky and Lego. His flagship keynote 'The Art of Being Brilliant' has been delivered to rave reviews around the world. He also delivers in schools – because the earlier you can embed the principles of positivity, the better. And speaking of schools, Andy is also the author of the best-selling children's series, 'Spy Dog'.

Andy was born in the same year that England won the football world cup. He is married to Louise and they have two grown-up children as well as an assortment of pets (dogs and pigs mostly, and maybe some goats eventually). Andy has done numerous TV and radio appearances. He has also set up the hugely successful '2%ers club', the UK's first, foremost and...err...only society for happy people.

His ambition is to be able to surf, brilliantly!

Andy can be contacted at andy@artofbrilliance.co.uk or you can check out his work at www.artofbrilliance.co.uk

 Illustrator: Amy Bradley aka Arty-Amy

Amy works as an Illustrator & Designer from her quirky studio in Uttoxeter, Staffordshire. Her dream in life truly is to create fun, colourful illustrations for everyone! And without a doubt, that dream really is coming true.

She has drawn pictures for as long as she can remember and now as a fully pledged adult she reckons she has the best job in the world. Every single one of her illustrations is hand drawn, making use of digital techniques to add colour, character and excitement!

Amy loves working on a variety projects, including picture books, educational projects, branding, packaging and licensing (to name a few!) Working with the likes of; The Art of Brilliance, Capstone, Crown House Publishing, Scholastic, ELC, Brewers Fayre and many more. Geee wiz!!

With clients from many corners of the world Amy is also a wannabe globetrotter!

Amy can be contacted at mail@amybradley.co.uk or you can check out her work at www.amybradley.co.uk